NATIONAL DEFENSE RESEARCH INSTITUTE

T0122925

From Stalemate to Settlement

Lessons for Afghanistan from Historical Insurgencies That Have Been Resolved Through Negotiations

Colin P. Clarke, Christopher Paul

Prepared for the Office of the Secretary of Defense

The research described in this report was prepared for the Office of the Secretary of Defense (OSD). The research was conducted within the RAND National Defense Research Institute, a federally funded research and development center sponsored by OSD, the Joint Staff, the Unified Combatant Commands, the Navy, the Marine Corps, the defense agencies, and the defense Intelligence Community under Contract W91WAW-12-C-0030.

Library of Congress Cataloging-in-Publication Data is available for this publication.

ISBN: 978-0-8330-8237-4

The RAND Corporation is a nonprofit institution that helps improve policy and decisionmaking through research and analysis. RAND's publications do not necessarily reflect the opinions of its research clients and sponsors.

Support RAND—make a tax-deductible charitable contribution at www.rand.org/giving/contribute.html

RAND® is a registered trademark

Cover image: British Royal Marines Brigadier Ed Davis (left), the commander of Task Force Helmand, shakes hands with Gen. Hakim Angar, the Helmand province chief of police, to commemorate the transition of lead security authority in Lashkar Gah district, Helmand province, Afghanistan, July 20, 2011 (British Royal Air Force photo by Sgt. Mitch Moore/Released).

© Copyright 2014 RAND Corporation

RAND OFFICES

SANTA MONICA, CA • WASHINGTON, DC
PITTSBURGH, PA • NEW ORLEANS, LA • JACKSON, MS • BOSTON, MA
DOHA, QA • CAMBRIDGE, UK • BRUSSELS, BE

www.rand.org

Preface

This report builds on previous RAND Corporation research on the demonstrated effectiveness of a variety of concepts for counterinsurgency. That earlier effort considered 71 insurgencies completed worldwide between 1944 and 2010. At the core of the current research is an analysis of the correlates and conditions of negotiated settlements in historical insurgencies. Thirteen of the 71 insurgencies examined ended with a mixed outcome through a negotiated settlement. The findings from these cases may hold implications for the current situation in Afghanistan.

This work will be of interest to defense analysts and military planners who are responsible for evaluating current U.S. operations and counterinsurgency efforts, especially those attempting to craft an end game for Afghanistan; to military and civilian decisionmakers with responsibility for Afghanistan; to academics and scholars who engage in historical research on counterinsurgency, insurgency, irregular warfare, or conflict resolution; and to students of contemporary and historical international conflicts.

Readers will also find the following RAND publications to be of interest:

- *Paths to Victory: Lessons from Modern Insurgencies*, Christopher Paul, Colin P. Clarke, Beth Grill, and Molly Dunigan (RR-291/1-OSD), 2013.
- *Paths to Victory: Detailed Insurgency Case Studies*, Christopher Paul, Colin P. Clarke, Beth Grill, and Molly Dunigan (RR-291/2-OSD), 2013.

- *Counterinsurgency Scorecard: Afghanistan in Early 2013 Relative to Insurgencies Since World War II*, Christopher Paul, Colin P. Clarke, Beth Grill, and Molly Dunigan (RR-396-OSD, 2013)
- *Victory Has a Thousand Fathers: Sources of Success in Counterinsurgency*, by Christopher Paul, Colin P. Clarke, and Beth Grill (MG-964-OSD), 2010.
- *Victory Has a Thousand Fathers: Detailed Counterinsurgency Case Studies*, Christopher Paul, Colin P. Clarke, and Beth Grill (MG-964/1-OSD), 2010.

This research was conducted within the International Security and Defense Policy Center of the RAND National Defense Research Institute, a federally funded research and development center sponsored by the Office of the Secretary of Defense, the Joint Staff, the Unified Combatant Commands, the Navy, the Marine Corps, the defense agencies, and the defense Intelligence Community.

For more information on the International Security and Defense Policy Center, see http://www.rand.org/nsrd/ndri/centers/isdp.html or contact the director (contact information is provided on the web page).

Contents

Figures and Tables

Figures

Tables

Summary

Using strategic narrative and case-study analysis, this research examined in depth 13 historical cases of insurgency that have been settled through negotiation and ended with a mixed outcome (that is, neither side completely won or completely lost). From these 13 cases, we distilled a "master narrative" for how conflicts reach a conclusion through a process of negotiated settlement. This "master narrative" does not follow the precise storyline of one specific insurgency; rather, it is distilled from many insurgencies. Using the factors detailed in the 13 case studies, we sought to identify commonalities in the progress toward a negotiated settlement. Again, the master narrative developed does not describe a specific path toward negotiated settlement, but it does seek to capture the essential ingredients and sequence of factors common to the 13 cases. After explaining how we developed the master narrative, we apply it to possible future directions for Afghanistan following the 2014 withdrawal of international troops.

The master narrative for negotiated settlements generally unfolds in seven steps, though not always in this exact order. First, after years of fighting, both sides in a conflict reach a state of war-weariness and settle into a mutually hurting military stalemate, in which the costs of escalating the conflict would be greater than the benefits of doing so for both sides. Second, after a stalemate has been reached and the belligerents recognize the futility of continued escalation, the insurgents are accepted as a legitimate negotiating partner. Once the government accepts the insurgents, the terms of a cease-fire can be discussed. This third step (cease-fire)—like step 2 before it—is highly dependent on the acquiescence of external powers, such as other countries involved or invested in the conflict. For example, if an active external supporter is pushing for continued conflict, it is likely that the negotiation process will end here.

If external actors refrain from further meddling, official intermediate agreements can be reached. This is the fourth step in the narrative. In the fifth step, power-sharing offers (including, for example, amnesty or elections) can further entice the insurgents to favor politics over armed struggle. Sixth, once the insurgents accept a power-sharing offer, the insurgency's leadership becomes more moderate, facilitating further progress by giving a voice to the politically minded cadre of the group. Seventh, and finally, third-party guarantors help guide the process to a close, acting as impartial observers or providers of security, economic and development aid, and other forms of assistance.

Figure S.1 outlines our master narrative for insurgencies that progress from conflict to negotiated settlement. Although only one of the 13 cases considered unfolded exactly according to this sequence, each case unfolded in a manner close enough to this narrative that it is a useful comparative tool for understanding how to reach negotiated settlements.

Figure S.1
Master Narrative for Reaching Negotiated Settlements

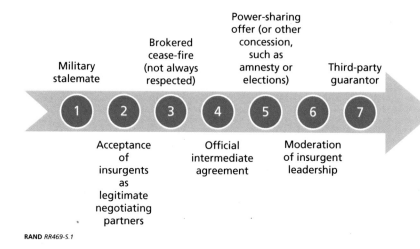

RAND RR469-S.1

Table S.1 shows which of the 13 cases passed through any the seven steps of the master narrative and in what order. The first row, for the Northern Ireland conflict, shows that the case progressed through all 7 steps in that order. Where steps occurred nearly simultaneously (as was the case for steps 2, 3, and 4 in the Congo case), this is denoted with the same number. Two things are noteworthy in the table. First, as is often the case with a master narrative, it perfectly described very few of the cases (only one, Northern Ireland, followed all steps in order). Second, most of the cases do include most of the master narrative steps, and predominantly in the specified order.

Recommendations

While it is still too early to tell whether the conflict in Afghanistan will end in a negotiated settlement, should this prove to be the case, it seems likely that the result of any negotiated settlement will be "mixed," with both the Afghan government and the Taliban making fairly major concessions to reach an agreement. Even if this is not the ultimate end game, it is still valuable to examine the combination of factors needed for a negotiated settlement so we can analyze whether or not it could be successful. Let us be clear, a mixed, negotiated settlement is not a *fait accompli*. Much can still happen between now and the final phase of the conflict in Afghanistan, especially if the force mix on the ground differs radically from the current force. The situation as it stands in 2013 is around step 2, which means that some combination of the approximately five remaining steps toward negotiated settlement still need to occur.

To reach a negotiated settlement, it helps if both sides have faced setbacks, neither side perceives unambiguous military victory as likely, external actors on both sides reduce their levels of support, and all external actors press for negotiated settlement (and at least one external actor is willing to act as a guarantor). Based on these criteria, prospects for a negotiated settlement in Afghanistan look reasonably good if the insurgents are unable to prevail militarily once the coalition withdraws, if insurgents' external supporters push for a negotiated settlement, and

Table S.1
The Master Narrative for Reaching Negotiated Settlements in 13 Selected Cases and Order of Steps

Case	Stalemate	Insurgents Accepted as Political Partners	Cease-Fires	Official Intermediate Agreements	Power-Sharing Offers	Moderation of Insurgent Leadership	Third-Party Guarantors
	1	2	3	4	5	6	7
Northern Ireland, 1969–1999	1	2	3	4	5	6	7
Yemen, 1962–1970	1	3	—	2	4	4	4
Philippines (Moro Islamic Liberation Front [MNLF]), 1971–1996	1	2	3	3	6	5	—
Lebanese Civil War, 1975–1990	1	4	2	3	7	6	5
Western Sahara, 1975–1991	1	4	2	4	—	3	6
Mozambique (Mozambican National Resistance [RENAMO]), 1976–1995	1	3	4	2	6	5	7
Indonesia (Aceh), 1976–2005	1	2	3	5	6	4	7
Kampuchea, 1978–1992	1	2	3	—	4	5	6
Bosnia, 1992–1995	1	4	2	2	4	—	6
Tajikistan, 1992–1997	1	2	4	3	5	5	7
Burundi, 1993–2003	1	2	4	3	5	5	7
Chechnya I, 1994–1996	1	3	2	3	5	—	—
Democratic Republic of the Congo (anti-Kabila), 1998–2003	1	2	2	2	6	5	7

if a third party can be found to act as an honest broker and provide peacekeepers.

With a stalemate largely achieved, the master narrative for reaching a negotiated settlement as applied to Afghanistan suggests that efforts are necessary to make progress toward the following (steps 2–5):

- *Step 2:* Co-opt the leadership on both sides and put sufficient pressure on respective parties (the United States on the Karzai government, Pakistan on the Taliban) to accept each other as legitimate negotiation participants.
  - *Substep 2:* Convince external powers to support peace rather than continued fighting.
- *Step 3:* Broker a cease-fire.
- *Step 4:* Make progress toward some type of official agreement.
- *Step 5:* Offer a power-sharing agreement: The promise of political legitimacy to the insurgent leadership must be a step in the process, not a measure of last resort.

Acknowledgments

We gratefully acknowledge Peter Lavoy and Chris Kolenda in the Office of the Assistant Secretary of Defense for Asian and Pacific Security Affairs; Timothy Bright, David Lowe, Louise Hoehl, Harvey Dennison, and Matt Schaffer in the Office of the Secretary of Defense, Cost Assessment and Program Evaluation; and James Dobbins, Seth Jones, Eric Peltz, and Olga Oliker at RAND.

We also wish to thank our reviewers, Georgetown University's Dan Byman and RAND's Paul Miller. The report benefited greatly from their thoughtful and thorough reviews and the insights and suggestions they provided.

Abbreviations

AFPAK	Afghanistan-Pakistan
ANSF	Afghan National Security Forces
APRP	Afghan Peace and Reintegration Program
CIRA	Continuity Irish Republican Army
COIN	counterinsurgency
DRC	Democratic Republic of the Congo
FARC	Fuerzas Armadas Revolucionarias Colombianas [Revolutionary Armed Forces of Colombia]
FDD	Forces for the Defense of Democracy
FRELIMO	Frente de Libertação de Moçambique [Mozambique Liberation Front]
GAM	Gerakan Aceh Merdeka [Free Aceh Movement]
HIG	Hezb-e-Islami Gulbuddin
IRA	Irish Republican Army
ISAF	International Security Assistance Force
LTTE	Liberation Tigers of Tamil Eelam
MNLF	Moro Islamic Liberation Front
NATO	North Atlantic Treaty Organization
PIRA	Provisional Irish Republican Army

RENAMO	Resistência Nacional Moçambicana [Mozambican National Resistance]
UN	United Nations
UTO	United Tajik Opposition

From Stalemate to Settlement: Lessons for Afghanistan from Historical Insurgencies That Have Been Resolved Through Negotiations

Introduction

Insurgency has been the most common form of armed conflict since at least the end of World War II. Over the past decade, scholars, observers, and theorists of insurgency and counterinsurgency (COIN)—amateur and professional alike—have fiercely debated the subject. While the emphasis on "how to win" in COIN is understandable, especially from the perspective of those engaged in the fighting, the historical record is definitive. Unambiguous military victory by either insurgents or counterinsurgents is far from the norm. Indeed, the data reveal that more than half of all insurgencies have been settled through negotiation. Yet, the question remains: What steps must be taken to reach a negotiated settlement?

There is an axiom in sports that dictates, "Play for the win on the road" but "Play for the tie at home." In COIN parlance, external actors are "on the road" and, thus, should "play for the win." But COIN is not soccer. Brokering a negotiated settlement that results in a mixed outcome—or "playing for a tie"—is likely the best-case scenario for the International Security Assistance Force (ISAF) in Afghanistan under current withdrawal plans. As Fotini Christia and Michael Semple suggested several years ago, "Time is short, and effective engagement with the Taliban could mean the difference between a protracted, unwinnable conflict and a pragmatic solution acceptable to both Washington and its Afghan allies."[1] Since then, time has grown shorter. Understanding which factors are important and which are not is crucial to shaping the current debate on an end-game strategy for Afghanistan.

This short report uses a thoughtful selection of case studies of insurgency to identify common steps taken in reaching negotiated settlements. Using strategic narrative and case-study analysis, it examines in depth 13 historical cases of insurgency that have been settled through negotiation and ended with a mixed outcome (with neither side completely winning or completely losing). By applying lessons learned from the resulting "master narrative," it applies the analysis to Afghanistan. The concluding section of the report discusses the implications for that conflict and provides recommendations for reaching a negotiated settlement.

How to Reach a Negotiated Settlement in Counterinsurgency Warfare

In June 2013, the Afghan Taliban opened a political office in Qatar to facilitate peace talks with the U.S. and Afghan governments. Negotiations between the United States and the group that sheltered al-Qaeda would have been unthinkable 12 years ago, but the reality today is that a negotiated settlement in Afghanistan is one of several possible end games facing the United States under the current withdrawal plan. And while it is one thing to reach the conclusion that the world's lone superpower must come to the table with an insurgency it had once hoped to extirpate, but the more difficult task is figuring out how to reach a negotiated settlement once all sides are seated at that table.

In a speech delivered on April 4, 2002, former U.S. President George W. Bush stoutly declared, "No nation can negotiate with terrorists."[2] He was certainly not the first standing president to make such a statement. More than a decade earlier, Ronald Reagan had

---

[1] Fotini Christia and Michael Semple, "Flipping the Taliban: How to Win in Afghanistan," *Foreign Affairs*, July–August 2009, p. 45.

[2] "Text of Bush Middle East Speech," ABC News, April 4, 2002.

declared that "there will be no negotiations with terrorists of any kind."[3] To be sure, not negotiating with terrorists is U.S. policy. Similar pronouncements have been put forward at various points by the leaders of Colombia, Turkey, Spain, the United Kingdom, and other countries.[4] But the fact of the matter is that governments and their high-ranking officials *do* negotiate with terrorists. They also negotiate with guerrillas, insurgents, and recognized war criminals. Moreover, while negotiating an end to an insurgency is a long and often arduous process, frequently beset by false starts and continued violence, a comprehensive analysis of historical cases that ended in settlement shows that most of these negotiations follow a similar path that can be generalized into a "master narrative."

The Notion of a Master Narrative

Strategic narrative is a useful frame for the history-theory relationship in qualitative, historical research and suggests that some stories and ways of constructing stories will promote theory building more than others, enabling researchers to cumulate knowledge more effectively.[5] "Master narrative," in this context, refers to a simple sequence of idealized steps that more or less accurately describes the historical progression of a certain kind of event. For example, when briefing our work on COIN,[6] we describe the "typical" Central or South American case. Such a case begins with a modest insurgency in the countryside. The government does not perceive the insurgency to be much of threat and treats it as a law-and-order problem, leaving it to the police.

---

[3] Jason Koebler, "Why Governments Should Negotiate with Terrorists," *U.S. News and World Report*, July 31, 2012.

[4] Harmonie Toros, "'We Don't Negotiate with Terrorists!' Legitimacy and Complexity in Terrorist Conflicts," *Security Dialogue*, Vol. 49, No. 4, August 2008, p. 408.

[5] Robin Stryker, "Beyond History Versus Theory: Strategic Narrative and Sociological Explanation," *Sociological Methods and Research*, Vol. 24, No. 3, February 1996.

[6] See Christopher Paul, Colin P. Clarke, Beth Grill, and Molly Dunigan, *Paths to Victory: Lessons from Modern Insurgencies*, Santa Monica, Calif.: RAND Corporation, RR-291/1-OSD, 2013c, and Christopher Paul, Colin P. Clarke, and Beth Grill, *Victory Has a Thousand Fathers: Sources of Success in Counterinsurgency*, Santa Monica, Calif.: RAND Corporation, MG-964-OSD, 2010b.

Police forces prove to be overmatched by the insurgency, which grows in strength. Alarmed by the increasing size of the insurgency and now feeling threatened, the government mobilizes its armed forces for internal security. The national army smashes the insurgency with disproportionate force, also devastating adjacent civilian populations. Over time, the insurgency recovers, but it now has much greater support from the population, and it now poses the most serious threat to the government yet.[7]

Figure 1 summarizes our master narrative for insurgencies that progress from conflict to negotiated settlement. And while not all of the cases we consider unfold exactly according to this sequence (in fact, only one does), each case unfolds in a manner close enough to this narrative that it is a useful comparative tool for understanding how to reach to negotiated settlements.

The narrative for the 13 historical cases examined for this research unfolds in the following seven steps. First, after years of fighting, both sides in a conflict reach a state of war-weariness and settle into a mutually hurting military stalemate.[8] Second, after a stalemate has been reached and the belligerents recognize the futility of continued escalation, the insurgents are accepted as a legitimate negotiating partner. Once the government accepts the insurgents, the terms of a cease-fire can be discussed. This third step, cease-fire—like step 2 before it— is highly dependent on the acquiescence of external powers, such as other countries involved or invested in the conflict. For example, if an active external supporter is pushing for continued conflict, it is likely that the negotiation process will end here.

---

[7] This is a master narrative for insurgencies in that part of the world. It encapsulates elements of several different struggles against insurgents and presents them in a generally characteristic sequence that suggests an important caution for future COIN forces. Of course, no actual Central or South American insurgency proceeded exactly in this way; the master narrative tells the story of many insurgencies without telling the precise story of any specific insurgency. We sought to identify a master narrative for progress toward negotiated settlement following the same formula. The master narrative developed for this report is not intended to describe any specific progress toward negotiated settlement, but it does seek to capture the essential ingredients and sequence characteristic to most of them.

[8] *Mutually hurting stalemate* refers to a stalemate in which both sides are suffering but neither side has enough of an advantage to escalate toward victory.

Figure 1
Master Narrative for Reaching Negotiated Settlements

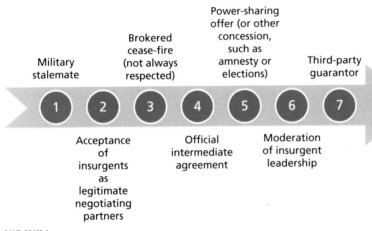

RAND RR469-1

If external actors refrain from further meddling, official intermediate agreements can be reached. This is the fourth step in the narrative. In the fifth step, power-sharing offers (including, for example,
amnesty or elections) can further entice the insurgents to favor politics
over armed struggle. Sixth, once the insurgents accept a power-sharing
offer, the insurgency's leadership becomes more moderate, facilitating
further progress by giving a voice to the politically minded cadre of
the group. Seventh, and finally, third-party guarantors help guide the
process to a close, acting as impartial observers or providers of security,
economic and development aid, and other forms of assistance.

Methods: Getting to a Master Narrative

Previous RAND Research: *Paths to Victory*
The RAND report *Paths to Victory: Lessons from Modern Insurgencies*
used detailed case studies of the 71 insurgencies begun and completed
worldwide between World War II and 2010 to analyze correlates of

success in COIN.[9] We used this comprehensive collection of modern insurgencies as the foundation for our examination of negotiated settlements.

We began with the 71 cases from our previous research. *Paths to Victory* identifies a subset of 59 of those cases as appropriate comparative cases, with the other 12 cases excluded as inappropriate comparisons because they were "fought against the tide of history"—specifically, they involved governments opposing the end of colonialism or the end of apartheid.[10]

Of these 59 core cases, 29 were resolved through negotiated settlement, and, of these 29 negotiated settlements, 13 were judged to have "mixed" outcomes. We chose to focus exclusively on negotiated settlements in cases with mixed outcomes because those in which one side or the other unambiguously prevailed have a different character, even when they ended in negotiations. We deliberately chose to eschew cases in which negotiations were simply the codification of military victory by one side because they tended to be negotiated capitulations, or negotiations regarding amnesty and demobilization, and served primarily to end fighting and minimize further bloodshed. In these cases, negotiations were not initiated because a stalemate had been reached and one side could not prevail through continued fighting. The 13 selected cases, shown in Table 1, were "mixed" by virtue of either one or both sides making major concessions in the same phase of the conflict—in most cases, the decisive phase.[11] In all 13 cases, what con-

---

[9] Note that although the study includes 71 detailed case studies, only 59 were considered "core" cases and informed the quantitative and comparative analyses. The excluded cases were "fought against the tide of history"; that is, they were cases in which the outcome was all but predetermined by exogenous global trends, such as the end of colonialism or the end of apartheid. Many of these "tide of history" cases are individually interesting and informative, but they make poor comparative cases because often quite well-designed and -executed COIN campaigns ultimately failed due to inexorable changes in their context. Full details can be found in Paul, Clarke, Grill, and Dunigan, 2013c.

[10] See Paul, Clarke, Grill, and Dunigan, 2013c, for a complete discussion.

[11] The case of Western Sahara is what is termed a "frozen conflict," which results when active armed conflict ends but the political framework to reach a negotiated settlement has not been finalized. Hence, the conflict remains "frozen" as is.

Table 1
Thirteen Cases of Negotiated Settlement, Mixed Outcome

Cases	Year	Outcome
Northern Ireland	1969–1999	Favoring COIN
Yemen	1962–1970	Favoring insurgents
Philippines (Moro Islamic Liberation Front [MNLF])	1971–1996	Favoring COIN
Lebanese Civil War	1975–1990	Favoring insurgents
Western Sahara	1975–1991	Favoring COIN
Mozambique (Mozambican National Resistance [RENAMO])	1976–1995	Favoring COIN
Indonesia (Aceh)	1976–2005	Favoring COIN
Kampuchea	1978–1992	Favoring insurgents
Bosnia	1992–1995	Favoring insurgents
Tajikistan	1992–1997	Favoring insurgents
Burundi	1993–2003	Favoring insurgents
Chechnya I	1994–1996	Favoring insurgents
Democratic Republic of the Congo (anti-Kabila)	1998–2003	Favoring insurgents

stituted a "major" concession and who (the COIN force or the insurgents) had the better of a mixed outcome largely depended on the distinct narrative of that case. While it is still too early to tell whether the conflict in Afghanistan will end in a negotiated settlement, this seems to be a possible outcome. With U.S. troops scheduled to withdraw in 2014, the task of blunting future insurgent offensives will be left to the Afghan National Security Forces (ANSF) and a residual U.S. force that provides training and assistance. There are no indications that U.S. forces will remain in Afghanistan in a capacity robust enough to move the conflict beyond its current stalemate and in favor of the Afghan government. Indeed, as things stand today, the United States is pushing for, and seems content with, a negotiated settlement to the war in Afghanistan, even if that means that the Afghan government (and, by extension, the U.S. government) must make significant compromises to bring the insurgents to the negotiating table. For these reasons, we believe that the result of any negotiated settlement will be "mixed," with both the Afghan government and the Taliban making fairly major concessions to reach an agreement. We explore these possibilities in greater detail toward the end of this report.

Developing the Master Narrative

Using existing case-study data from *Paths to Victory*, along with data collected for *Throwing in the Towel: Why Insurgents Negotiate* and some additional research on each of the 13 cases, the master narrative for negotiated settlements followed from the thoughtful collective and individual examinations of the narratives for each case.[12] Strategic narrative compels a researcher to construct history as both a path-dependent action sequence and as context, in a manner that comports with clearly articulated theoretical understanding.[13]

The Master Narrative

As noted in the introduction, unambiguous military victory by either insurgents or counterinsurgents is far from the norm. Of the 71 cases analyzed in *Paths to Victory*, slightly more than half (n = 37) were resolved through negotiated settlement. And while the literature is rich with studies on the causes of negotiated settlements,[14] postconflict and peace-building ramifications,[15] and strategies chosen by governments

---

[12] Paul, Clarke, Grill, and Dunigan, 2013c; Colin Clarke, *Throwing in the Towel: Why Insurgents Negotiate*, doctoral dissertation, Pittsburgh, Pa.: University of Pittsburgh, January 2013.

[13] Stryker, 1996, p. 310.

[14] For example, Virginia Page Fortna, "Where Have All the Victories Gone? War Outcomes in Historical Perspective," paper presented at the American Political Science Association annual meeting, Chicago, Ill., September 2, 2004b. See also Barbara F. Walter, *The Successful Settlement of Civil Wars*, Princeton, N.J.: Princeton University Press, 2001.

[15] Monica Duffy Toft, *Securing the Peace: The Durable Settlement of Civil Wars*, Princeton, N.J.: Princeton University Press, 2009; Roy Licklider, "The Consequences of Negotiated

seeking to terminate a conflict through settlement,[16] there has been little research on the step-by-step process of reaching a negotiated settlement and even less on a sequence, or master narrative, to explain how such agreements are reached.

The sections that follow offer detailed definitions of each step in our master narrative. We then discuss our sample historical cases and explain how they informed the narrative's development.

Step 1: Military Stalemate and War-Weariness

Conflicts become "ripe for resolution" in cases of a mutually hurting stalemate. This occurs when the adversaries in a conflict find themselves locked in a state from which they are unable to escalate to victory, and this deadlock is painful to both of them (though not necessarily to equal degrees or for the same reason).[17] As parties to the conflict grow increasingly war-weary, they become more amenable to finding ways out of the conflict, including negotiated settlement. In other words, when an attractive alternative is capable of creating a situation that is believed to be superior to remaining locked in stalemate, a mutually acceptable solution becomes possible.[18]

This step occurred in all 13 cases and was the first step in each case's progression to a negotiated settlement. It is important to note that moving on to step 2 can take time, and conflicts vary. In both Northern Ireland and the Philippines (MNLF), a stalemate was reached early

---

Settlements in Civil Wars, 1945–1993," *American Political Science Review*, Vol. 89, No. 3, September 1995; Caroline A. Hartzell, "Explaining the Stability of Negotiated Settlements to Intrastate Wars," *Journal of Conflict Resolution*, Vol. 43, No. 1, February 1999.

[16] Patrick Johnston, "Negotiated Settlements and Government Strategy in Civil War: Evidence from Darfur," *Civil Wars*, Vol. 9, No. 4, December 2007.

[17] I. William Zartman, "Dynamics and Constraints in Negotiations in Internal Conflicts," in I. William Zartman, ed., *Elusive Peace: Negotiating an End to Civil Wars*, Washington, D.C.: Brookings Institution Press, 1995, p. 11.

[18] In the conflict resolution literature, the concept of a mutually hurting stalemate has been criticized as vague and difficult to operationalize. We acknowledge this point but feel that the issue of stalemate was so critical to so many of the cases that it warranted inclusion and significant attention. War-weariness, too, can seem like a post hoc judgment but nevertheless played an important role in reaching what Zartman refers to as a "ripe moment" for resolution.

on, but it took decades to reach a negotiated settlement in both cases. Accordingly, for the belligerents to transition away from further escalation, neither side can feel that its most significant interests are threatened. Most importantly, to move forward in the process, each side must·convince the other that it accepts the other's legitimacy.[19]

Step 2: Acceptance of Insurgents as Legitimate Negotiating Partners or Non-Adversaries

Talks with insurgents have many risks, ranging from political embarrassment to encouraging more violence and even strengthening the group's capacity for bloodshed.[20] Achieving this initial step is often critical to actually beginning negotiations, but can be complicated when the insurgency is characterized by genocide, mass atrocities, or internecine ethnic conflict. However, in both Bosnia and Burundi, the government was able to accept the insurgents as legitimate negotiating partners, despite the high levels of violence in these cases. To the extent that legitimacy and popular recognition are a conferral of enhanced status to former political pariahs, this is a necessary evil in the negotiation process.[21]

When insurgents are never seriously accepted as legitimate negotiating partners, the result is often a "frozen" conflict. In Western Sahara, the Moroccan government negotiated for an independence referendum that it never held—and likely never intended to hold—because it never really accepting the insurgents as legitimate partners. Finally, as mentioned earlier, as a substep between steps 2 and 3, external powers must acquiesce to negotiations. If an active external supporter is pushing for continued conflict, meaningfully passing through steps 2 or 3 is much more difficult, if not impossible.

---

[19] Louis Kriesberg, *Constructive Conflicts: From Escalation to Resolution*, Lanham, Md.: Rowman and Littlefield, 2003, p. 204.

[20] Daniel Byman, "Talking with Insurgents: A Guide for the Perplexed," *Washington Quarterly*, Vol. 32, No. 2, April 2009.

[21] Leonard Weinberg, Ami Pedahzur, and Ari Perliger, *Political Parties and Terrorist Groups*, London: Routledge, 2009, p. 144.

Step 3: Brokered Cease-Fires (Not Always Respected)

Cease-fires should be viewed as incremental steps in the negotiation process that may provide a temporary respite from the violence, thus opening space for the parties to maneuver politically and appeal to their constituencies. Although cease-fires are sometimes derided as opportunities for insurgents to rest, rearm, and recuperate (and many times they are just that), they are also opportunities to expose parties that are inimical to negotiation and can lead to the splintering of adversary groups or expose potential spoilers to a peace process. An unwelcome byproduct of insurgent group splintering is that members of the "rump" group that emerges from the "mother" organization can be even more violent than the group that spawned it, "responding to the imperative to demonstrate their existence and signal their dissent," according to as Audrey Kurth Cronin.[22]

Key characteristics of cease-fires are that these agreements operate on the basis of reciprocity and mutual deterrence.[23] If respected, reciprocity (even if driven by deterrence) can serve as a confidence-building measure, which, in turn, can initiate an opening for more substantive talks. In Tajikistan, a United Nations (UN)–sponsored cease-fire provided an opening for the government and the United Tajik Opposition to sign the Peace and National Reconciliation Accord in 1997.

Step 4: Official Intermediate Agreements

Official intermediate agreements, even if not viewed as successful at the time, provide a show of good faith, create goodwill, foster credibility, and serve as building blocks to later negotiations. Intermediate agreements do not always include the actual belligerents to the conflict, relying instead on the acquiescence of external actors. If undertaken

---

[22] Audrey Kurth Cronin, "How al-Qaida Ends: The Decline and Demise of Terrorist Groups," in Robert J. Art and Kenneth Waltz, eds., *The Use of Force: Military Power and International Politics*, Lanham, Md.: Rowman and Littlefield, 2009, p. 515.

[23] Virginia Page Fortna, *Peace Time: Cease-Fire Agreements and the Durability of Peace*, Princeton, N.J.: Princeton University Press, 2004a, p. 37.

unilaterally, negotiations can cause a rift between allies that, for political reasons, may be unable to negotiate.[24]

These types of agreements reduce the chances of sharp escalation. For example, in Mozambique, the 1984 Nkomati Accord stipulated that, in return for denying the African National Congress sanctuary in Mozambique, South Africa would cease to support RENAMO. This helped deescalate the conflict and paved the way for the Rome Accords less than a decade later, in 1992. Another example is the 1962–1970 insurgency in Yemen, in which the Jeddah Pact between the Saudis and the Egyptians led to a temporary calm in fighting and a decline in Egyptian troop levels. Although the agreement subsequently collapsed, it demonstrated that compromise was possible.

Step 5: Power-Sharing Offers

When the government makes an offer to share power with insurgents, it can entice them with a measure of legitimacy and provide the opportunity to change their calculus from violence to politics. Such offers can take a variety of forms, including elections, guaranteed ministry seats, cabinet posts in a future government, the integration of military forces, or written agreements to grant and observe territorial autonomy.[25]

The primary assumption buttressing the theory of power-sharing is the idea that political engineering can lead to the creation of a democratic political system that is able to withstand the many forces gnawing at the newly created institutions of government.[26]

In the consociational approach to power-sharing, elites cooperate after elections to form multiethnic coalitions and manage conflict, while the integrative approach to power-sharing encourages parties to create coalitions *before* elections, focusing on the creation of broadly

---

[24] Peter C. Sederberg, "Conciliation as Counter-Terrorist Strategy," *Journal of Peace Research*, Vol. 32, No. 3, 1995.

[25] Michael G. Findley, "Bargaining and the Interdependent States of Civil War Resolution," *Journal of Conflict Resolution*, Vol. 57, No. 5, October 2013.

[26] Timothy D. Sisk, *Power Sharing and International Mediation in Ethnic Conflicts*, Washington, D.C.: United States Institute of Peace, 1996, p. 77.

inclusive but majoritarian governments.[27] In an example of the former, the Taif Agreement of 1989 cemented the notion of a "shared existence" among the various sectarian groups in Lebanon and altered the balance of power.[28]

Step 6: Moderation of Insurgent Leadership

With more contact and dependence on moderate members, insurgent groups will be more likely to pull away from "extreme strands" and move toward a position that makes concession possible.[29] Talks can change the opinions of constituents while strengthening more moderate elements of an insurgency, increasing the chances of successful negotiation.[30] Sometimes, exogenous events can lead to moderation in a group's leadership. Conditions in the Second Congo War changed when Laurent Kabila was assassinated and his son, Joseph, took over. Joseph had a greater interest in political compromise, beginning negotiations early on in his presidency and working to reach a settlement.

But what if moderates never emerge? All too often, the more moderate elements of an insurgent group (e.g., those willing to negotiate with the opposition) are isolated and harangued as capitulators. Especially in conflicts in which much blood has been shed, there are significant gains to be made from adhering to an extreme position. Moderates can be sidelined easily, cast as weak and unprepared to lead. As such, engaging moderates is never easy, though it behooves the COIN force to identify these individuals and elevate them to a position of power, where possible.

Step 7: Third-Party Guarantors

Unless there is an impartial third party that is trusted by both sides and capable of overseeing implementation, the lack of mutual confi-

---

[27] Sisk, 1996, p. 35.

[28] Perhaps more importantly, tens of thousands of Syrian troops deployed to Lebanon in October 1990 and crushed the remaining resistance.

[29] Dean Pruitt, "Negotiation with Terrorists," *International Negotiation*, Vol. 11, No. 2, 2006.

[30] Byman, 2009, p. 136.

dence between formerly warring parties often causes agreements to falter and conflict to be renewed.[31] The UN has served as a third-party guarantor of security and governance during myriad negotiated settlements, including in Kampuchea, Bosnia, and Mozambique, to name a few. Caroline Hartzell has found that negotiated settlements that provide institutional guarantees against the security threats perceived by antagonists are more likely to have staying power.[32] Indeed, according to this line of reasoning, the international community's promised deployment of peacekeepers can motivate adversaries to reach a negotiated settlement by fostering an environment of security, thus mitigating the risk to belligerents who choose peace.[33]

Sequences in the Individual Cases

Table 2 shows which of the seven steps of the master narrative each of the 13 cases passed through and in what order. For example, in the Northern Ireland conflict, the case progressed through all seven steps in the same order as our master narrative. Where steps occurred nearly simultaneously (as was the case for steps 2, 3, and 4 in the Democratic Republic of the Congo), this is denoted by the use of the same sequence number. Three points are noteworthy. First, as is often the case with such approaches, our master narrative perfectly describes very few of the cases. (Only one, Northern Ireland, followed all the steps in order.) Second, most of the cases *do* include all the master narrative steps, and predominantly in the specified order. Third, the issue of time horizons is critical to understanding the sequence. In several cases, attempts to negotiate occurred early in the conflict but a final resolution was not reached for years, or sometimes decades. All conflicts proceeded at a

---

[31] James Shinn and James Dobbins, *Afghan Peace Talks: A Primer*, Santa Monica, Calif.: RAND Corporation, MG-1131-RC, 2011.

[32] Hartzell, 1999.

[33] Caroline A. Hartzell and Matthew Hoddie, *Crafting Peace: Power-Sharing Institutions and the Negotiated Settlement of Civil Wars*, University Park, Pa.: Penn State University Press, 2007, pp. 62–63.

Table 2
The Master Narrative for Reaching Negotiated Settlements in 13 Selected Cases and Order of Steps

Case	Stalemate	Insurgents Accepted as Political Partner	Cease-Fires	Official Intermediate Agreements	Power-Sharing Offers	Moderation of Insurgent Leadership	Third-Party Guarantors
Northern Ireland,1969–1999	1	2	3	4	5	6	7
Yemen, 1962–1970	1	3	—	2	4	4	4
Philippines (MNLF), 1971–1996	1	2	3	3	6	5	—
Lebanese Civil War, 1975–1990	1	4	2	3	7	6	5
Western Sahara, 1975–1991	1	4	2	4	—	3	6
Mozambique (RENAMO), 1976–1995	1	3	4	2	6	5	7
Indonesia (Aceh), 1976–2005	1	2	3	5	6	4	7
Kampuchea, 1978–1992	1	2	3	—	4	5	6
Bosnia, 1992–1995	1	4	2	2	4	—	6
Tajikistan, 1992–1997	1	2	4	3	5	5	7
Burundi, 1993–2003	1	2	4	3	5	5	7
Chechnya I, 1994–1996	1	3	2	3	5	—	—
Democratic Republic of the Congo (anti-Kabila), 1998–2003	1	2	2	2	6	5	7

different pace, and context can be affected by a range of events, both internal and external. Negotiations can take on a life of their own, but if policymakers hope to expedite the process, they must assess progress at each of the seven steps and evaluate the feasibility of ultimately reaching an agreement.

Next, we examine each case and the individual sequence it followed, beginning with a detailed discussion of Northern Ireland. Where cases deviated from the master narrative, this deviation is explained.

Extended Example: Northern Ireland, 1969–1999

Table 3 presents the sequence of the master narrative in Northern Ireland. Because it conforms to our master narrative, we analyze this case as an extended example, detailing steps 1–7.

Step 1: Military Stalemate and War-Weariness

Contrary to what many casual observers of "The Troubles" in Northern Ireland believe, the war between the PIRA and the British Army reached a mutually hurting stalemate just a few years into the 30-year conflict. Although the COIN force maintained superior military capabilities throughout the conflict, in the first years of the fighting, British forces suffered woefully from "out-of-date" intelligence.[34] Inaccurate intelligence was a major contributing factor in the lead-up to a disastrous operation on January 30, 1972, when British paratroopers opened fire on unarmed civil rights marchers who had organized a protest.[35] The incident was labeled "Bloody Sunday."

Sectarian lines were drawn and remained stout. Exclusively Catholic areas, such as Creggan, Brandywell, and the Bogside in Derry, along with large pockets of West Belfast, became veritable no-go zones for the COIN force. The inability to enter these areas prevented the

---

[34] Bradley W. C. Bamford, "The Role and Effectiveness of Intelligence in Northern Ireland," *Intelligence and National Security*, Vol. 20, No. 4, December 2005, p. 583.

[35] Richard English, *Armed Struggle: The History of the IRA*, Oxford, UK: Oxford University Press, 2003, p. 151.

Table 3
Northern Ireland, 1969–1999 (Outcome: Mixed, Favoring COIN)

Step	Narrative
1	British COIN forces launched Operation Motorman to breakup no-go zones in predominantly Catholic neighborhoods where the insurgents held sway. After 1972, the conflict settled into a stalemate—the insurgents, paramilitaries, and COIN forces could not escalate to gain a military advantage.
2	Backchannel talks between the British government and the upper echelons of the insurgent leadership signaled the willingness to accept the Provisional Irish Republican Army (PIRA) as a legitimate negotiating partner, although an actual agreement would take decades.
3	A cease-fire was agreed to toward the end of 1974, although it collapsed amid insurgent accusations that the British were never serious about discussing "structures of disengagement" that could lead to a COIN force withdrawal. Paramilitary violence also contributed to the end of the armistice.
4	The 1985 Anglo-Irish Agreement was an official intermediate agreement that, while not able to bring the conflict to an end, did succeed in persuading the insurgents to engage politically.
5	The Downing Street Declaration of 1993 enshrined important principles of a power-sharing arrangement and brought the insurgents even closer to renouncing violence.
6	By the mid-1990s, the insurgent leadership made a conscious effort to shift resources away from its armed wing and toward its political arm, Sinn Fein. When violence ebbed, Sinn Fein prospered at the polls. Electoral success had a moderating effect on PIRA leadership.
7	Under the stewardship of George Mitchell, the United States played a major role as a third-party guarantor, helping craft the framework that led to the 1998 Good Friday Agreement and the end of the 30-year insurgency.

British from obtaining reliable intelligence, further complicating the war effort and increasing the chances for another Bloody Sunday. To overcome this obstacle, the COIN force launched Operation Motorman on July 31, 1972, an offensive that included 27 infantry battalions and two armored battalions of 22,000 regular troops and 5,300 reserve soldiers from the Ulster Defence Regiment.[36]

---

[36] M. L. R. Smith and Peter R. Neumann, "Motorman's Long Journey: Changing the Strategic Setting in Northern Ireland," *Contemporary British History*, Vol. 19, No. 4, December 2005.

In 1972, a total of 497 people were killed as a result of the conflict in Northern Ireland. Following Motorman, the insurgents never
again killed more than 138 people in a single year.[37] Politically, London
could reasonably endure a couple hundred deaths per year in perpetu-
ity. Successive British governments felt comfortable with this number,
as the violence never again reached a level that created enough pressure
for the COIN force, at least in strategic terms, to radically reconsider
its stance.

The stalemate persisted and was eventually recognized in formal
statements by both sides. Secretary of State for Northern Ireland Peter
Brooke, in remarks delivered to a press agency in November 1989,
admitted that the PIRA and the British were deadlocked in a military
stalemate.[38] The insurgents were also cognizant of this reality. According to Tim Pat Coogan, an unnamed PIRA member described the
situation as such: "Our aim is to create such psychological damage to
the Brits that they'll withdraw, sick of the expense, the hassle, the cof-
fins coming back to England. But we know we can't defeat them in
a military sense, no more than they can beat us. So there's kind of a
stalemate."[39]

Step 2: Acceptance of Insurgents as Legitimate Negotiating Partners
From the earliest phase of the conflict, secret backchannel talks took
place between members of the insurgency and officials in the British
government. These talks gained momentum once a stalemate had been
recognized. In a demonstration of the COIN force's acceptance of the
insurgents as legitimate negotiating partners, British ministers, including then–Secretary of State for Northern Ireland William Whitelaw,
met with PIRA leaders Gerry Adams and Martin McGuinness in mid-
1972 to discuss a possible resolution to the conflict.[40] Although the

---

[37] English, 2003, p. 379.

[38] English, 2003, p. 247.

[39] Quoted in Tim Pat Coogan, *The IRA*, New York: Palgrave, 2000, p. 604.

[40] Andrew Mumford, *Puncturing the Counterinsurgency Myth: Britain and Irregular Warfare
in the Past, Present, and Future*, Carlisle, Pa.: Strategic Studies Institute, U.S. Army War College, September 2011, p. 12.

talks collapsed, they solidified the notion of the insurgent leaders as legitimate interlocutors. Other actors had signaled a willingness to engage, too. As early as 1974, the government in Dublin was engaged in backchannel talks with various elements of the Ulster Volunteer Force.

These backchannel talks were a critical step in the process. As a result of the continuous push and pull of these track II diplomacy initiatives, both sides knew who their partners were and, perhaps more importantly, who their partners were not.[41] Although the belligerents talked about peace for a long time, the conflict trudged along for years. Nevertheless, backchannel talks and attempts at informal diplomacy between Nationalists, Unionists, and the British government laid the groundwork and incrementally set the parameters of how future negotiations unfolded. From that perspective, they are important to analyze.

The Sunningdale Agreement of 1973 was the most public attempt at political reconciliation in the first decade of the conflict, and one that included competing interests on all sides—PIRA, the Social Democratic and Labour Party, the Ulster Unionist Party, the Democratic Unionist Party, and the governments in both London and Dublin. The terms of the agreement included a devolved legislative assembly, all-Ireland institutional cooperation and consultation, and a human rights provision.[42] Sunningdale is remembered for accomplishing what had been unthinkable up to this point in the conflict in the zero-sum atmosphere of Northern Ireland politics: It succeeded in alienating *both* Unionists and Nationalists alike, as each thought their side compromised too much in the deal. This was clearly something that those in favor of Sunningdale had anticipated. Indeed, the COIN force had done its due diligence in the lead-up to the agreement. To marginalize potential spoilers, British forces arrested and detained elements of the Belfast Brigade's leadership who were thought to be completely opposed to any form of negotiation.

---

[41] Tony Novosel, *Northern Ireland's Lost Opportunity: The Frustrated Promise of Political Loyalism*, London: Pluto Press, 2013.

[42] English, 2003, p. 165.

By targeting the hardliners in the group, the British sought to shape the insurgent leadership in a way that would make the PIRA more amenable to reaching a deal. According to Ed Moloney, the failure of Sunningdale "seemed to symbolize to the outside world the addiction of the parties in Northern Ireland to their ancient quarrel and spoke to an almost inherited inability on the part of the belligerents to entertain reasonable solutions."[43] The result was a coordinated strike by the unionist Ulster Workers' Council and, on the Nationalist side, increased friction between Sinn Fein and the Social Democratic and Labour Party.

Step 3: Brokered Cease-Fires (Not Always Respected)

After insurgents have been accepted as legitimate negotiating partners, the next step is to seek a "ripe moment," a way to break the chain of tit-for-tat violence. The 1974–1975 cease-fire was agreed to as both sides hoped to escape the futility of bloody sectarian violence. Some of the more moderate insurgent leaders had high hopes for what could be considered the first serious opening for a potential breakthrough in talks since the conflict began six years earlier. But not everyone in the PIRA's inner circle was on board with the idea.

Gerry Adams believed that the cease-fire would lead only to negative outcomes for the PIRA. Adams refused to discuss any moves toward a cease-fire unless the deal would be a starting point to focus on "structures of disengagement" that would ultimately lead to a British withdrawal from Northern Ireland.[44] Adams argued that any cessation in fighting at this point in the conflict would allow the COIN force the time needed to resupply and reorganize its intelligence apparatus. Specifically, the insurgent leadership cadre grew concerned that a cease-fire would enable a Loyalist offensive directed at Catholic civilians, particularly in Belfast.[45]

---

[43] Ed Moloney, *A Secret History of the IRA*, New York: W. W. Norton and Company, 2002, pp. 141–142.

[44] Moloney, 2002, p. 143.

[45] Moloney, 2002, p. 145.

The once-promising cease-fire broke down and gave way to the rise of sectarian death squads, such as the Shankhill Butchers. Not to be outdone, the PIRA responded with an intensified campaign of its own, also directed at civilians. The return to violence had a profound impact on Adams, who became convinced that the British had negotiated in bad faith. Accordingly, in a series of articles published in *An Phoblacht*, Adams argued persuasively that what was needed was "active abstentionism," coupled with a focus on building alternative structures of governance to provide critical services to the minority Catholic population in the north. The provision of services would be the responsibility of Sinn Fein.

This period in the PIRA's history has been identified as the turning point at which the political wing received equal consideration with the military activities of the group. But the move was subtle and, more importantly, it displayed Adams's skill for appeasing the group's hardline elements, whom he sought to convince that politics and armed struggle were not mutually exclusive after all. Rather, increasing political support through the vehicle of Sinn Fein would enable the insurgents to intensify and sustain the war effort. Moreover, even though Sunningdale was roundly rejected as an abject failure to bring the sides closer together, significant (albeit not always visible) progress had been made since then.

By the mid-1980s, the belligerents recognized the growing morass into which the conflict had slipped. The insurgents had already been accepted as legitimate negotiating partners and a cease-fire was agreed to, despite its failure to take root. The next step was to work toward an official intermediate agreement that would demonstrate good faith and serve as a confidence-building measure for the continuation of dialogue.

Step 4: Official Intermediate Agreements

The Anglo-Irish Agreement of 1985 made remarkable strides toward peace and was viewed as "an accord that was profoundly to alter the framework within which the Irish Republican Army (IRA) were to operate in subsequent years."[46] Essentially, the agreement gave the Republic of Ireland a continuing and consultative role in the affairs of Northern Ireland, with increased responsibility for border security. In an example of what conflict resolution scholar Stephen John Stedman has dubbed the "departing train" strategy of managing spoilers in a peace process, the governments in London and Dublin agreed that the peace process would continue without the PIRA and would cultivate opportunities for those parties that chose to pursue peace.[47]

The insurgent leadership correctly realized that it was being marginalized by these negotiations. Shortly after the Anglo-Irish Agreement was signed, Gerry Adams stated that it had been "designed to isolate and defeat republicans."[48] Adams recognized that a move toward political inclusion was a necessary next step to avoid being shut out of the political framework that London and Dublin appeared to be building without PIRA involvement. Active abstentionism was not producing any tangible gains for the insurgents, but the policy had been a longstanding tradition in the group's lore.

Those who favored abandoning the bullet for the ballot were regarded as naïve at best, traitorous at worst. The PIRA's position on abstention, or refusing to sit for political office in any parliament (of the Republic of Ireland, Northern Ireland, or England), is best summarized by J. Bowyer Bell, who believed that, in the eyes of most PIRA members, sitting in parliament or participating in electoral politics "was not only an invitation to corruption, a tainted tactic already proven sterile, but also, and most important, outrageous immorality."[49] To be sure, the PIRA emerged due, in large part, to a disagreement

---

[46] English, 2003, pp. 240–241.

[47] Stephen John Stedman, "Spoiler Problems in Peace Processes," *International Security*, Vol. 22, No. 2, Fall 1997.

[48] English, 2003, pp. 240–242.

[49] J. Bowyer Bell, *The Secret Army: The IRA*, rev. 3rd ed., New Brunswick, N.J.: Transaction Publishers, 1997, p. 344.

over this very issue.[50] Yet, the peace process appeared to be moving forward, with or without the PIRA.

In 1986, at a General Army Convention in County Donegal, Adams lobbied those in attendance that selected members of the Irish republican movement should make a foray into politics south of the border by taking a seat in the Dáil Éireann, the Irish parliament.[51] Unlike previous insurgent leaders who argued that the IRA drop its policy of abstentionism to contest seats in all three parliaments (Leinster House, Stormont, and the House of Commons in Westminster), Adams eschewed such an ambitious move in favor of a pragmatic effort to elevate the importance of Sinn Fein, the insurgency's political wing. The result was predictable. Ruairi O'Bradaigh and other veteran IRA hardliners walked out of the meeting and went on to found Republican Sinn Fein, along with a splinter military wing that came to be known as the Continuity Irish Republican Army (CIRA).[52]

Step 5: Power-Sharing Offers

The frequency of secret backchannel talks among all participants in the conflict in Northern Ireland helped move the parties away from violence and toward resolution. To the public, the Downing Street Declaration of 1993 was a joint British-Irish statement crafted by British Prime Minister John Major and his Irish counterpart, Albert Reynolds. However, as we now know, "what made the Downing Street document exceptional was that it was modeled on ideas and concepts evolved, initiated, and developed in a secret dialogue whose instigator [Gerry

---

[50] In October 1969, the IRA Army Council voted against maintaining the traditional policy of abstention in the parliaments of Dublin, Belfast, and London. In addition to what many future PIRA members felt was a failure on the part of the IRA (or the Official IRA, as it would be referred to following the 1969 split) to protect the Catholic population from violence, the Army Council's decision to reverse its position on the long-standing policy of abstention was the primary motivation for Sean MacStiofain and his allies to split from the Cathal Goulding–led IRA.

[51] Moloney, 2002, p. 288.

[52] Moloney, 2002, p. 289. In 1996, the CIRA would claim responsibility for the deadly bombing of a hotel in Enniskillen, County Fermanagh, which was a direct effort to sabotage the peace talks that were under way at the time.

Adams] was the head of the political organization pledged to over-throw the principle [of consent] by gun and bomb."[53]

The main tenets of the Downing Street Declaration that caused the biggest stir were the principle of self-determination and the principle of consent. These principles were indispensable to the insurgents' view of what a power-sharing arrangement should entail. Both of these ideas were conceptualized in paragraph 4 of the document, which stated,

> The British Government agree that it is for the people of the island of Ireland alone, by agreement between the two parts respectively, to exercise their right of self-determination on the basis of consent, freely and concurrently given, North and South, to bring about a united Ireland, if that is their wish. They reaffirm, as a binding obligation that they will for their part introduce the necessary legislation to give effect to this, or equally to any measure of agreement on future relationships in Ireland which the people of Ireland may themselves freely so determine without external impediment.[54]

In other words, it would be the right of the people of Ireland, both North and South, to determine their fate. John Hume, leader of the Social Democratic and Labour Party, thought that the declaration was an explicit refutation of the PIRA's call to violence. The British openly declared no self-interest—economic, political, or military—in the affairs of Ireland. But what angered Irish republicans above all else—especially the politically active and influential members in prison—was that the document failed to include an overt commitment by the British government to withdraw its forces from Northern Ireland.[55]

The promise of power-sharing helped the insurgents to mature politically. As PIRA violence ebbed, Sinn Fein's electoral success flowed. There was an inverse relationship between PIRA violence, especially as the civilian death toll rose, and Sinn Fein's ability to win votes.

---

[53] Moloney, 2002, p. 286.

[54] Joint Declaration of 15 December 1993 (Downing St. Declaration), 1993; para. 4.

[55] Moloney, 2002, p. 413.

The republicans' constituency was tired of the violence and demonstrated this fatigue at the polls. By the 1990s, the political element of the PIRA's organization had become more than just an "add-on" to armed struggle.

Step 6: Moderation of Insurgent Leadership

With electoral success came increased legitimacy. Each bombing was now met with a loss in popular support. Adams had initially sold the hardliners in the organization on the notion that politics were a mere smokescreen and negotiations were nothing more than a ruse to expose the British government's lack of commitment to the process. The PIRA's leadership looked back on the cease-fire of 1974–1975 and vowed that never again would the group commit to a cease-fire until "the Brits declared for withdrawal."[56] In practice, even the phrase cease-fire had become so discredited that it was rarely used.

By 1994, the war had been going on for 25 years. The political "stepping stones" of the Anglo-Irish Agreement (1985) and the Downing Street Declaration (1993) galvanized the necessary political capital for both sides to break the impasse. While Adams and a small group of advisers were negotiating the political terms of a cease-fire, the Army Council worked out the details on the military side. For the PIRA, the terms of a cease-fire included a complete halt to recruiting, military training, targeting activity, and intelligence-gathering for operational activities.[57] These prohibitions applied to PIRA units in Northern Ireland and in the Republic. In return, British COIN forces would temporarily halt police actions, including surveillance, imprisonment, and harassment of the insurgents. When the vote on whether to support the cease-fire was put before the Army Council, five members were in favor, one abstained, and one voted against it.[58] Adams, once the fiercest advocate of physical force as *the only* way ahead, voted for peace. He could now be aptly characterized as a moderate.

---

[56] Coogan, 2000, p. 396.

[57] Moloney, 2002, p. 425.

[58] Moloney, 2002, p. 426.

What caused Adams to finally accept that violence no longer had a place in Northern Ireland, and when did this change occur exactly? First, Adams recognized that the PIRA and British COIN forces had been stuck in a military stalemate for quite some time, lamenting that "the IRA were able to block the imposition of a British solution but were unable to force the British to withdraw."[59] Second, he felt that his organization was now in a much more powerful bargaining position than ever before. The entire incentive structure had changed by the 1990s, and the ever-opportunistic Adams believed that Sinn Fein/PIRA could gain considerable ground on issues high on the group's wish list, including police reform, prisoner release, and, most importantly, placing Irish republicans in the upper echelons of government.[60] Third, and finally, the relationship between the nationalists and their loyalist counterparts had undergone major changes. The PIRA spent so much of its energy focusing on the British that, at times, the loyalists seemed to be nothing more than a nuisance that could be dealt with at a later point.

Step 7: Third-Party Guarantor

By the mid-1990s, the political dynamics on all sides had changed. With the support of a President (Bill Clinton) who "leaned toward green rather than the orange," U.S. involvement went beyond that of a mediator and took the shape of a guarantor. Despite disagreement between hardliners and the Army Council, Adams had cultivated undeniable clout for the PIRA on the international stage and had achieved unparalleled traction within the group's upper echelons. In 1995, former Maine Senator George Mitchell was appointed U.S. Special Envoy for Northern Ireland. He subsequently crafted the Mitchell Principles, six ground rules that would facilitate a final agreement to the conflict. Among these ground rules were the total disarmament of all paramilitary organizations, an agreement to abide by democratic and

---

[59] Gerry Adams, *Before the Dawn: An Autobiography*, New York: William Morrow and Co., 1996, p. 58.

[60] English, 2003, p. 309.

exclusively peaceful means of resolving political issues, and a pledge to engage in all-party negotiations in good faith.

In 1998, the insurgency in Northern Ireland officially came to an end with the signing of the Good Friday Agreement. This historical agreement was the culmination of 30 years of conflict in Northern Ireland. Fifteen years after the signing of this historic peace deal, all parties to the conflict have remained focused on politics, and a lasting peace has settled in throughout the country, pockmarked by only episodic acts of violence practiced by fringe groups and criminals.[61] The PIRA laid down its arms and stepped aside for Sinn Fein, completing a process that had begun years earlier.

By opening the political system to the insurgents, the British government was able to end the conflict. With a changed political status quo, the PIRA now had a stake in the political future of its own country. Furthermore, the group would be held accountable, not only to the government it was now a part of but also to its constituency. Failing to deliver would have serious consequences. Allowing the PIRA to transition into politics also drew a clandestine group out into the open and forced it to remain transparent and abide by the same rules and laws that governed other political parties. Finally, by including the insurgents in the government, the British were able to abdicate the role of third-party guarantor. The future of Northern Ireland, for better or worse, would now be determined by its citizens and their respective political representatives and institutions.

---

[61] See John Horgan and John F. Morrison, "Here to Stay? The Rising Threat of Violent Dissident Republicanism in Northern Ireland," *Terrorism and Political Violence*, Vol. 23, No. 4, 2011. See also Martyn Frampton, *The Return of the Militants: Violent Dissident Republicanism*, London: International Centre for the Study of Radicalisation, King's College London, 2010.

Twelve Additional Cases of Historical Insurgency Settled Through Negotiation

This section continues the discussion of the 13 cases, though in an abbreviated format. For each of the remaining 12 cases, we present a summary table describing how the master narrative played out in each case, followed by a brief discussion of the distinctive features of the case.

Yemen, 1962–1970

Table 4 details the steps on the way to a settlement in the Yemen case. The Jeddah Pact was an agreement that resulted from mediation talks between Egyptian President Nasser and Saudi King Faisal and included a pledge by the Saudis to stop providing support to the royal-

Table 4
Yemen, 1962–1970 (Outcome: Mixed, Favoring Insurgents)

Step	Narrative
1	In the battle between the royalists, supported by Saudi Arabia, and the republicans, backed by Gamal Abdel Nasser's Egypt, the conflict in North Yemen reached a stalemate by 1963. Though it had superior firepower, the COIN force was unable to reduce support for the insurgency or limit the royalists' freedom of action.
2	In 1965, Egyptian President Nasser and Saudi King Faisal concluded the Jeddah Pact, which committed the Saudis to stop supplying the royalists in return for a pledge from the Egyptians to withdraw from Yemen.
3	The Jeddah Pact resulted in a temporary respite from conflict and allowed the two sides to attempt to reach a further compromise on the creation of a provisional government. Fighting resumed in December 1965, when a power-sharing deal fell through, but the belligerents had demonstrated a willingness to accept each other as a serious party to a negotiated settlement.
4 and 5	In May 1970, with regional and international pressure mounting, a compromise was reached in which the republicans agreed to establish a more moderate government.
5	The Saudis acted as a third-party guarantor by shepherding the insurgents and COIN forces through negotiations.
6	The insurgency was resolved when the government guaranteed representation for the insurgents, who achieved significant concessions on political autonomy.

ists. In return, Nasser agreed that the Egyptians would withdraw their forces from Yemen within a year. The immediate result of the pact was a lull in the fighting, though this peace proved tenuous.

Perhaps an even more significant result was a decline in Egyptian troop levels, down to 20,000. Still, with tensions between the royalists and the republicans still quite tangible, the two sides were unable to move forward with the creation of a provisional government by the end of 1965. Changing regional dynamics shifted the balance of power. The United Kingdom would withdraw from South Yemen just as the Soviets would pledge continued support to Nasser in his quest to extend Egyptian influence throughout the region.[62] Although the Jeddah Pact fell apart, it proved that progress was possible: The conflict might not be as intractable as it once seemed. Even after Jeddah, it took another five years before international pressure helped push the conflict into a new phase. Eventually, the government acquiesced and agreed to guarantee political representation for the insurgents.

Philippines (MNLF), 1971–1996

Table 5 uses the master narrative as a framework to describe the progression to settlement between the Philippine government and the MNLF. In September 1996, the Philippine government and the insurgents finalized a negotiated settlement. Per the terms of the agreement, the MNLF was granted a degree of autonomy within the territory as outlined in the Tripoli Agreement.[63] The Autonomous Region for Muslim Mindanao would remain part of the national territory of the Republic of the Philippines, and the country's president would retain supervisory control over the regional governor. The 1996 agreement also required the government to provide amnesty to approximately 7,000 insurgents.[64] Many former MNLF members have successfully reintegrated back into society, including the political system.

---

[62] David M. Witty, "A Regular Army in Counterinsurgency Operations: Egypt in Yemen, 1962–1967," *Journal of Military History*, Vol. 65, No. 2, April 2001.

[63] Hartzell and Hoddie, 2007, pp. 130–131.

[64] Rachel M. Rudolph, "Transition in the Philippines: The Moro National Liberation Front (MNLF), the Moro Islamic Liberation Front (MILF) and Abu Sayyaf's Group (ASG)," in

Table 5
Philippines (MNLF), 1971–1996 (Outcome: Mixed, Favoring COIN)

Step	Narrative
1	Fighting between the Government of the Republic of the Philippines and the MNLF reached a stalemate approximately five years into the war, as the government slowly lost control in the insurgent-held territory of Mindanao and Sulu.[a]
2	Failing to gain ground after employing a combination of both hard- and soft-power tactics, including economic aid programs and political concessions, the COIN force eventually warmed to the idea of negotiating with the insurgents.[b]
3	In 1976, the Organization of the Islamic Conference helped bring the warring parties together to sign the Tripoli Accord.
4	As a result of the accord, a cease-fire was declared in three provinces and ten cities, though the armistice failed to take root.
5	In 1986, Philippine President Ferdinand Marcos was ousted in a coup and replaced by Corazon Aquino, a far more moderate leader than Marcos and one determined to end the conflict with the MNLF.[c]
6	In January 1987, the government and the insurgents reached an agreement in which the MNLF relinquished its goal of independence for the country's Muslim regions. In turn, the insurgents were offered—and accepted—a renewed measure of autonomy to govern their own affairs. It took another ten years before an accord was signed between the MNLF and the government of the Philippines in September 1996.

[a] Anthony James Joes, *Guerrilla Warfare: A Historical, Biographical, and Bibliographical Sourcebook*, Westport, Conn.: Greenwood Press, 1996, pp. 167–180.

[b] Rudolph, 2008, p. 152.

[c] As in the Democratic Republic of the Congo, it was not the peace process itself that was responsible for new leadership, but progress in the peace process did help influence the moderate members of the Philippine government who were interested in bringing the conflict to an end.

While accepting the insurgents as legitimate negotiating partners and conceding to certain MNLF demands, the government was able to quell one of several antigovernment rebellions in its territory. By appearing willing to negotiate with the government, the MNLF was subjected to both verbal and physical attacks from other Muslim insurgent groups in the Philippines, including both the Moro Islamic Lib-

Anisseh Van Engeland, and Rachel M. Rudolph, *From Terrorism to Politics*, Burlington, Vt.: Ashgate, 2008, p. 155.

eration Front and the Abu Sayyaf Group. Although the MNLF settled, both the Moro Islamic Liberation Front and the Abu Sayyaf Group are still actively perpetrating political violence against the government.

Lebanese Civil War, 1975–1990

Table 6 shows the narrative progression in Lebanon toward a power-sharing settlement that ended the civil war. The most significant moment in Lebanon's 15-year civil war was the signing of the Taif Accords in 1989, a peace agreement that officially ended the conflict. A tripartite commission of Saudi Arabia, Morocco, and Algeria helped broker the agreement, with the Saudis playing the biggest role. Essentially, the Taif Accords cemented the notion of a "shared existence"

Table 6
Lebanese Civil War, 1975–1990 (Outcome: Mixed, Favoring Insurgents)

Step	Narrative
1	By the time of Israel's invasion of Lebanon in 1982, the civil war had already been raging for seven years and the parties to the conflict had reached a stalemate long before that. The Lebanese army and government were paralyzed from political deadlock, while the country broke down along ethnic and sectarian lines, earning the nickname "the Militia Republic."
2	In the late 1970s, the Syrians dispatched thousands of soldiers to Lebanon to exert Damascus' influence. Following Syria's intervention, the Palestinians, the Lebanese National Movement, and the Lebanese Front agreed to a cease-fire, bringing the fighting to a temporary halt.
3	In 1982, an official intermediate agreement led the Palestine Liberation Organization to move its base from Lebanon to Tunisia.
4	The first major breakthrough in the 15-year insurgency raging in Lebanon was the signing of the Taif Accords in 1989, a peace agreement that officially ended the Lebanese civil war.
5	A tripartite commission of Saudi Arabia, Morocco, and Algeria helped broker the agreement, with the Saudis playing the leading role.
6	In the group's first display of pragmatism, Hizballah dropped its prerequisite of establishing Lebanon as an Islamic state and joined the government in Beirut.
7	As a result of the Taif Accords, the presidency was still reserved for a Christian and the prime minister would still be a Sunni Muslim, but now the prime minister would be responsible not to the president but to the legislature, as in a traditional parliamentary system.

among the various sectarian groups in Lebanon and altered the balance of power by taking some authority away from the Maronites.[65] Other changes initiated by the agreement were an increase from 108 to 208 members of parliament, divided equally among Muslims and Christians.

As part of the Taif Accords, which became official when the parties in agreement signed the Document of National Understanding on September 21, 1990, all militias in the country *except* Hizballah were to disarm.[66] Because it held a unique role as a "resistance force" fighting the Israelis in southern Lebanon, Hizballah was allowed to retain its weapons. In October 1990, Syria deployed tens of thousands of troops to Lebanon, occupied the presidential palace, and expelled General Michel Aoun. In 1991, Lebanon and Syria signed the Treaty of Brotherhood, Cooperation, and Coordination, which laid the groundwork for Syrian occupation of the country for the next 15 years.

Western Sahara, 1975–1991

Table 7 describes the steps from the master narrative that were present and those that were absent in settlement negotiations in Western Sahara—negotiations that were often less than sincere on the part of the Moroccan government.

Although the Settlement Plan brought about an end to active fighting between the COIN force and the insurgents, it failed to bring about a total resolution of the conflict. Even after the agreement, the Moroccan government was consistently accused of human rights abuses in the region, while most forms of protest were extirpated quickly and often through force. To increase Moroccan influence in Western Sahara, the government has pursued a policy of "Moroccanization," effectively transplanting Moroccan settlers while resettling native Sahwaris in Morocco. Continuing disagreement about the composition of

---

[65] Elizabeth Picard, *Lebanon: A Shattered Country*, New York: Holmes and Meier, 2002, p. 157.

[66] The actual peace agreement signed as part of the Taif Accords has been referred to in the literature as "the National Accord Document for Lebanon," "the Document of National Understanding," and "the Document of National Reconciliation." All three terms refer to the same document.

Table 7
Western Sahara, 1975–1991 (Outcome: Mixed, Favoring COIN)

Step	Narrative
1	After nearly a decade of on-again, off-again fighting with the Popular Front for the Liberation of the Saguia el Hamra and Rio de Oro (Polisario) movement in Western Sahara, Moroccan COIN forces constructed a system of defensive sand walls that essentially locked the conflict in a stalemate by the mid-1980s.[a]
2	Over the next several years, low-level fighting continued amid negotiations and diplomatic skirmishes over a cease-fire. The COIN force and the insurgents announced their tentative acceptance of a UN-proposed cease-fire toward the end of 1988.
3	In the conflict's first hint at moderation by leaders on both sides, Moroccan forces agreed to withdraw from disputed territory and hold a referendum on the self-determination of Western Sahara.
4	The Moroccan government eventually accepted the insurgents as a legitimate negotiating partner over the course of the next three years, during which the sides mapped out the implementation of the referendum plan.
5	An official intermediate agreement in the form of the Settlement Plan laid out concrete terms of the future referendum, including an expression of self-determination that would ultimately lead to full independence or the integration of Western Sahara into Moroccan territory.
6	The Settlement Plan also afforded for the deployment of a third-party guarantor, the UN Mission for the Referendum in Western Sahara.[b]
7	In the end, without international pressure forcing the Moroccan government to follow through, there was no referendum on power-sharing. The conflict remains "frozen" to this day.[c]

[a] Paul Staniland, "Defeating Transnational Insurgencies: The Best Offense Is a Good Fence," *Washington Quarterly*, Vol. 29, No. 1, Winter 2005–2006, p. 33.

[b] William J. Durch, "Building on Sand: UN Peacekeeping in the Western Sahara," *International Security*, Vol. 17, No. 4, Spring 1993.

[c] Stephen Zunes and Jacob Mundy, *Western Sahara: War, Nationalism, and Conflict Irresolution*, Syracuse, N.Y.: Syracuse University Press, 2010.

the electorate in a potential referendum has prevented the implementation of government reforms. Even decades after the signing of the cease-fire agreement, numerous false starts have prevented Morocco and the Sahrawi Arab Democratic Republic from being able to reach an agreement about the definitions and criteria for inclusion and exclusion of potential electors. Accusations of insincerity are rampant and trust between the two sides is lacking. While the two sides initially agreed that the electorate would be determined by a 1974 census of Western Sahara when it was still under Spanish control, Morocco subsequently insisted that voter rolls be expanded to include up to 150,000 people from Western Saharan tribes that had migrated to Morocco decades earlier.[67] As international attention waned, the conflict succumbed to the inertia of inattention and remains "frozen" to this day.

Mozambique (RENAMO), 1976–1995

Table 8 shows the narrative progression in Mozambique toward a settlement with RENAMO insurgents. The General Peace Agreement that formally ended the Mozambican civil war established an electoral system based on the principle of proportional representation and led to the stipulation that, to obtain a seat in the assembly, a party must receive a minimum percentage of countrywide votes, with no less than 5 percent and no more than 20 percent.[68] The negotiations to end the war were brokered in part by the Community of Sant'Egidio, an Italian Catholic charity organization that helped bring the opposing sides to the table. As one of several third-party guarantors, Italy arranged more than $400 million in financial support to help fund Mozambique's military and political reform efforts.[69]

The Supervision and Control Commission consisted of representatives from Mozambique Liberation Front (FRELIMO) and RENAMO, as well as special envoys from Italy, Portugal, France, Britain, and the United States and was granted dispute resolution authority and responsibility for coordinating subsidiary agencies, including the Cease-Fire Commission, the Commission for the Reintegration of Demobilizing Military Personnel, and the Joint Commission for the Formation of the Mozambican Defense Force.[70] With the adoption

---

[67] International Crisis Group, *Western Sahara: Out of the Impasse*, Middle East/North Africa Report No. 66, Cairo and Brussels, June 11, 2007.

[68] Hartzell and Hoddie, 2007, p. 30.

[69] Hartzell and Hoddie, 2007, p. 53.

[70] Chris Alden, "The UN and Resolution of Conflict in Mozambique," *Journal of Modern African Studies*, Vol. 33, No. 1, March 1995, p. 105.

Table 8
Mozambique (RENAMO), 1976–1995 (Outcome: Mixed, Favoring COIN)

Step	Narrative
1	In this postcolonial struggle between insurgents from RENAMO and the governing FRELIMO, neither side was able to marshal enough firepower to gain an advantage over the other. By 1983, the insurgents controlled most of the countryside and boasted a force of nearly 20,000 fighters.[a] With the capital under siege, the COIN forces decided to make a deal.
2	On March 16, 1984, Mozambique and South Africa signed the Nkomati Accord on Non-Aggression and Good Neighbourliness. The crux of the agreement stipulated that, in return for denying the African National Congress sanctuary in Mozambique, South Africa would cease its support for RENAMO. As the most powerful actor in the region, South Africa's decision to curb its support for Mozambican insurgents allowed the process to progress from step 2 to step 3.
3	The government recognized the insurgents as legitimate negotiating partners for the first time in 1990. Direct talks between RENAMO and the COIN force took place that year, even amid escalating violence on both sides.
4	By 1992, with external support absent and all sides of the conflict suffering from the legacy of decades of war, a cease-fire was agreed upon.
5	With a cease-fire in place, both RENAMO and FRELIMO made strides away from the more extreme strands of their respective organizations.
6	The cease-fire and apparent moderation of leaders in both the government and insurgency paved the way for the Rome Peace Accords. Also known as the General Peace Agreement, the framework enabled a transition to democratic multiparty elections, the assembly and demobilization of troops, the formation of new armed forces, the reintegration of demobilized combatants, and the resettlement of refugees and internally displaced persons.[b]
7	As part of the agreement, the UN Operation in Mozambique peacekeeping force deployed to monitor the transition period and provide stability during elections.

[a] William G. Thom, *African Wars: A Defense Intelligence Perspective*, Calgary, Alb.: University of Calgary Press, 2010, p. 106.

[b] Andrea Bartole, Aldo Civico, and Leone Gianturco, "Mozambique—Renamo," in Bruce W. Drayton and Louis Kriesberg, eds., *Conflict Transformation and Peacebuilding: Moving from Violence to Sustainable Peace*, London: Routledge, 2009, p. 149.

of UN Security Council Resolution 797 in December 1992, the UN Mission in Mozambique was created to monitor the transition period.

Indonesia (Aceh), 1976–2005

Table 9 describes the progression to settlement in Aceh province in Indonesia. In August 2005, after nearly three decades of ongoing conflict, the Helsinki Accords produced a memorandum of understanding between the government of Indonesia and the Free Aceh Movement, otherwise known as Gerakan Aceh Merdeka (GAM). The GAM waged a prolonged insurgency against the Indonesian state in a conflict that claimed between 12,500 and 15,000 lives over its duration. The election of Susilo Bambang Yudhoyono as president of Indonesia in late 2004 and the worldwide focus on Indonesia that resulted from the tsunami during this time period served to rejuvenate the peace process, which had stalled since the Cessation of Hostilities Agreement in 2003.

The Aceh Monitoring Mission—composed of the European Union, Switzerland, Norway, and the five member states of the Association of Southeast Asian Nations—worked as a facilitator between the belligerents in the conflict. The roles and responsibilities of the mission extended to such issues as human rights, legislative reform, amnesty regulation, and watching for violations of the memorandum of understanding. Meanwhile, the reintegration process was designed to ensure the economic facilitation of ex-combatants, pardoned political prisoners, and war-affected civilians.

Although the agreement is generally considered a success, the situation in the Indonesian province remains fragile largely because the Helsinki Accords did not include civilian militia groups. The military-backed Pembela Tanah Air (Defenders of the Homeland) still maintains a robust presence across the province. Left outside of the parameters of the peace process, the group was not required to demobilize or disarm and has since acted as a potential spoiler of stability in Aceh by threatening and intimidating ex-GAM fighters returning to their local villages.

Table 9
Indonesia (Aceh), 1976–2005 (Outcome: Mixed, Favoring COIN)

Step	Narrative
1	Although this conflict began in 1976, the GAM spent much of this time in a dormant phase, reemerging to fight the Suharto government at various points. Each time, the insurgents were beat back into submission, though Indonesian COIN forces were never able to fully extirpate the GAM.
2	In 1999, buoyed by the active and passive support of the Acehnese population, the insurgents went on the offensive in an attempt to break the stalemate.[a] But rather than attempt to crush the GAM with overwhelming firepower, as the counterinsurgents had done so often in the past, the Indonesian government softened its approach and recognized some legitimate grievances held by the insurgents. Following two decades of conflict, the government finally recognized the GAM as a legitimate negotiating partner and unilaterally granted Aceh special autonomy to apply Islamic law while simultaneously promising to investigate past human rights abuses.
3	In 2000, the Indonesian government discussed possible terms of a referendum on Aceh's status and entered into cease-fire negotiations with the GAM. Despite the initial success of the cease-fire, fighting flared up again shortly after it was announced.
4	Insurgent leaders grew more moderate by late 2004, perhaps driven by pragmatism on what was possible to achieve. GAM leaders and the government in Jakarta engaged in secret talks about a potential peace agreement. Talks were put on hold following the devastation wrought by the December 2004 tsunami, although many accounts of the conflict suggest that this natural disaster made both sides more willing to bring about an end to the conflict.[b]
5	An official intermediate agreement between the belligerents was cemented in August 2005. Known as the Helsinki Agreement, or the Memorandum of Understanding Between the Government of the Republic of Indonesia and the Free Aceh Movement, the memo included provisions on a range of issues, including disarmament, amnesty, and human rights.
6	After the Helsinki Agreement, the insurgents formed local political parties, and elections for local government posts in Aceh were held in December 2006. A former GAM strategist was elected governor, underlining the dramatic transformation brought about by the peace. Minor infighting among former rebels continued, but there were no major outbreaks of violence or return of insurgency.
7	Per the terms of the memorandum of understanding, the European Union assumed the role of a third-party guarantor, both in its pledge to monitor the agreement and as the primary source of funding behind the Aceh Monitoring Mission.

[a] Shane Joshua Barter, "Resources, Religion, Rebellion: The Sources and Lessons of Acehnese Separatism," *Small Wars and Insurgencies*, Vol. 19, No. 1, March 2008, p. 41.

[b] International Crisis Group, *Aceh: A New Chance for Peace*, Asia Briefing No. 40, Jakarta and Brussels, August 15, 2005.

Kampuchea, 1978–1992

Table 10 shows how the settlement in Kampuchea did and did not adhere to the steps in the master narrative. The Paris Conference on Cambodia produced the Agreements on a Comprehensive Political Settlement of the Cambodia Conflict, signed in October 1991. The Supreme National Council comprised the four main Cambodia factions and their armed wings: the Government of the State of Cambodia and the Cambodian People's Armed Forces, the Party of Democratic Kampuchea and the National Army of Democratic Kampuchea, the Khmer People's Liberation Front and the Khmer People's National Liberation Armed Force, and the United National Front for an Inde-

Table 10
Kampuchea, 1978–2002 (Outcome: Mixed, Favoring Insurgents)

Step	Narrative
1	Vietnam invaded Kampuchea in December 1978, and the counterinsurgents reached a stalemate soon after arriving in country. The insurgents enjoyed external support, including sanctuary, and once the Vietnamese forfeited the popular support of the population, their forces were marked as occupiers. This signaled the twilight of Vietnam's significance as an external actor in the conflict. By 1989, the COIN forces were prepared to hand off security operations to a proxy regime and its own well-armed military forces.[a]
2	In the summer of 1989, the four main Cambodian parties and representatives from more than a dozen other countries began negotiations to reach a settlement, which included terms of the Vietnamese withdrawal and the shape of a future government.
3	By October 1991, moderate leaders had emerged and signaled a willingness to sign a comprehensive settlement, which was concluded with the Paris Peace Agreement.
4	One of the results of the Paris Conference was that it bestowed upon the UN full authority to supervise a cease-fire, in addition to language that spoke to repatriation and the disarmament of factional armies.
5	Following the signing of the Paris Peace Agreement, Cambodia began to prepare for free and fair elections.
6	In 1993, the UN Transitional Authority in Cambodia assumed administration of Cambodia.

[a] Albert Grandolini, Tom Cooper, and Troung, "Cambodia, 1954–1999; Part 3," ACIG.org Indochina Database, January 25, 2004.

pendent, Neutral, Peaceful, and Cooperative Cambodia and the National Army of Independent Kampuchea.

The agreements had three main parts: the Agreement on a Comprehensive Political Settlement of the Cambodia Conflict; the Agreement Concerning the Sovereignty, Independence, Territorial Integrity and Inviolability, Neutrality, and National Unity of Cambodia; and the Declaration on the Rehabilitation and Reconstruction of Cambodia. The agreements also established the UN Transitional Authority in Cambodia, which had a mandate that covered human rights, responsibility for ensuring free and fair elections, repatriation and resettlement of refugees and internally displaced persons, security-sector reform, and a host of other civil and military matters. The transitional authority was unique in the comprehensiveness of its mandate and in that it was one of the few times the UN had assumed administrative authority over a sovereign member state.[71]

Bosnia, 1992–1995

Table 11 shows the narrative progression in Bosnia toward a settlement that ultimately favored the insurgents, the side supported by the North Atlantic Treaty Organization (NATO). The conflict ended with the Agreement for Peace in Bosnia and Herzegovina, also known as the Dayton Agreement or the Dayton Accords. The agreement resulted from a negotiated settlement that laid out the terms for peace in the war-torn Balkans while providing a roadmap for a return to normalcy. Dayton sought to succeed where the Vance-Owen plan had failed several years earlier, though coordinating and implementing the civilian aspects of Dayton proved extremely difficult.[72]

War-weariness had set in, and by 1995, the Serbs realized that continued conflict was unsustainable, especially as Western military involvement ramped up. NATO airpower had convinced Slobodan

---

[71] Centre for International Cooperation and Security, "Disarmament, Demobilisation, and Reintegration (DDR) and Human Security in Cambodia," Bradford, UK: University of Bradford, July 2007, p. 4.

[72] James Dobbins, John G. McGinn, Keith Crane, Seth G. Jones, Rollie Lal, Andrew Rathmell, Rachel M. Swanger, and Anga R. Timilsina, *America's Role in Nation-Building: From Germany to Iraq*, Santa Monica, Calif.: RAND Corporation, MR-1753-RC, 2003, p. 94.

Table 11
Bosnia, 1992–1995 (Outcome: Mixed, Favoring Insurgents)

Step	Narrative
1	Although a stalemate was reached early on in the conflict, NATO airpower helped the Bosnian Croats and Bosnian Muslims push President Slobodan Milosevic and the better-trained, better-equipped Bosnian Serbs to the brink.[a] Continuous fighting on multiple fronts strained Serb resources and, coupled with NATO airpower, helped convince Milosevic to seriously consider negotiations.
2	In March 1994, the Washington Agreement was signed, bridging the Croat-Muslim divide and unifying on-again, off-again allies in a united front against the insurgents
3	As part of the Washington Agreement, the Croats and Muslims agreed to a cease-fire.
4	The belligerents eventually accepted each other as legitimate negotiating partners, which culminated in the Dayton Peace Accords in December 1995.[b]
5	Power-sharing meant two political-territorial divisions, the Federation of Bosnia-Herzegovina and Republika Srpska, which left the insurgents with their own territory and functioning government, with the capital in Banja Luka.
6	The UN Mission in Bosnia and Herzegovina was established in 1995 and tasked with a range of postconflict functions, from law enforcement to police reform.

[a] R. Craig Nation, *War in the Balkans, 1991–2002*, Carlisle, Pa.: Strategic Studies Institute, U.S. Army War College, August 2003.

[b] Laura Silber, and Alan Little, *Yugoslavia: Death of a Nation*, New York: Penguin Books, 1995, pp. 369–377.

Milosevic to quit while he could, but it could do little to sort out political realities in the immediate aftermath of the war. According to Christopher Chivvis, "The ensuing peace was correspondingly tenuous, especially given that the political factions that had driven the conflict on all sides were not eliminated and would continue to pursue their war aims in peacetime."[73]

The agreement created two separate entities within Bosnia and Herzegovina: the Bosniak-Croat Federation and the Republika Srpska. Each entity maintained its own standing army. A new central govern-

---

[73] Christopher S. Chivvis, "The Dayton Dilemma," *Survival*, Vol. 52, No. 5, October–November 2010, p. 49.

ment was established, with power-sharing provisions and guarantees of Bosnian-Croat-Serb representation, coupled with a rotating presidency and bicameral legislature.[74] The Dayton Agreement has held firm in Bosnia, with continued gains in security and the economy over immediate post-war levels, though sectarianism and nationalist rhetoric still plague national politics.

Tajikistan, 1992–1997

Table 12 shows the narrative progression in Tajikistan toward a settlement that ultimately favored the insurgents. Step 2 in this process, the acceptance of the insurgents as legitimate negotiating partners, was the result of exhaustive track II diplomacy—specifically, the Inter-Tajik Dialogue, overseen by Russian scholar Gennady I. Chufrin and former U.S. diplomat Harold H. Saunders. The group met frequently and moved through five separate stages before devising ways to implement their plan. The third step in the process, uncovering the underlying dynamics of the relationship and discerning avenues to change these dynamics, was critical to the success of the initiative.[75]

Even more important than the role of track II diplomacy, however, was the role of the region's strongest power, Russia. As noted earlier, if an active external supporter is pushing for continued conflict, it is likely that any negotiation process will fail. Early on in the conflict, Russia's main priority was to protect its near-abroad by restoring erstwhile power structures enervated by the collapse of the Soviet Union. Several years into the conflict, Moscow was less concerned with installing Soviet-era apparatchiks and more interested in containing the conflict. Russian pressure on Dushanbe to reach a negotiated settlement was a major driver in the Tajik government's agreement to the terms of the National Reconciliation Accord.

---

[74] Hartzell and Hoddie, 2007, p. 148.

[75] Kriesberg, 2003, pp. 246–247.

Table 12
Tajikistan, 1992–1997 (Outcome: Mixed, Favoring Insurgents)

Step	Narrative
1	The Tajik government and its associated security forces battled the United Tajik Opposition (UTO) for control of the capital, Dushanbe. With neither side able to gain the upper hand, a stalemate settled in toward the end of 1992, when the insurgents established secure bases in the mountainous areas north and east of the capital, as well as rear bases in Afghanistan.[a]
2	In 1993, the United States and Russia sponsored the Inter-Tajik Dialogue track II diplomacy initiative.[b] Russia's role as an external power was essential to the Tajik government's acceptance of the insurgents.
3	In June 1997, the insurgents and the Tajik government signed the Peace and National Reconciliation Accord, an agreement that legally recognized the insurgent-led UTO as a legitimate political party.[c]
4	An armistice was established as part of the Peace and National Reconciliation Accord.
5	The Peace and National Reconciliation Accord led to the outline of a power-sharing agreement. Under the terms of the arrangement, the Tajik government agreed to grant the UTO 30 percent of government posts at the national and regional levels.[d]
6	In the lead-up to the 1999 elections, the tone of leaders from both the UTO and the Tajik majority softened, in an effort to present themselves as moderates.
7	Following elections, a UN observer mission helped shepherd along the peace process.[e]

[a] Nasrin Dadmehr, "Tajikistan: Regionalism and Weakness," in Robert I. Rotberg, ed., *State Failure and State Weakness in a Time of Terror*, Washington, D.C.: Brookings Institution Press, 2003.

[b] Harold H. Saunders, "Sustained Dialogue in Managing Intractable Conflict," *Negotiation Journal*, Vol. 19, No. 1, January 2003, pp. 87–88.

[c] Dov Lynch, "The Tajik Civil War and Peace Process," *Civil Wars*, Vol. 4, No. 4, 2001.

[d] Gregory Gleason, "The Politics of Counterinsurgency in Central Asia," *Problems of Post-Communism*, Vol. 49, No. 2, March–April 2002, p. 6.

[e] R. Grant Smith, "Tajikistan: The Rocky Road to Peace," *Central Asian Survey*, Vol. 18, No. 2, 1999.

Burundi, 1993–2003

Table 13 shows the extent to which the progress of the Burundi settlement adhered to the master narrative, describing some of the distinctive features of movement to successful negotiations in that case.

To break the deadlock of stalled negotiations, Nelson Mandela was designated as a special mediator for the conflict in 1999. Mandela succeeded in negotiating an agreement between the warring parties in August 2000 that allowed for the establishment of a transi-

Table 13
Burundi, 1993–2003 (Outcome: Mixed, Favoring Insurgents)

Step	Narrative
1	The ethnic violence between the Hutu majority and the Tutsi minority erupted following elections in 1993, with tens of thousands killed in a single week. A stalemate followed, with elements of the Tutsi-dominated army killing Hutu fighters and vice versa, leading to a massive refugee crisis and spillover violence throughout the region.[a]
2	In an attempt to break the five-year stalemate, Tutsi leaders engaged in talks with Hutu rebels, though with little success. Still, by the late 1990s, each side realized that the other was a permanent reality, and the belligerents tacitly accepted each other as legitimate negotiating partners. Insurgent intransigence and the reluctance of the Tutsi-led military to reach a peace agreement with the Hutu intelligentsia that dominated the Forces for the Defense of Democracy (FDD) was a major obstacle to further progress.
3	With the signing of the Lusaka accord, support for the FDD decreased. An ebb in the broader regional conflict meant that arms and funding for the Burundi rebels also dried up.
4	The government and the FDD reached a cease-fire agreement in late 2002, but the belligerents continued to fight and the agreement fell apart.
5	In a power-sharing deal designed to serve as a cornerstone to a negotiated settlement, the FDD renounced violence and demobilized its fighters in return for ministry positions, diplomatic posts, and local government control. In addition, the rebels were seeking to obtain nearly 40 percent of command posts in the army as part of any comprehensive peace agreement.
6	The Hutu National Liberation Forces continued to fight, but the core Hutu leadership and a significant portion of fighters agreed to negotiations.
7	Finally, in April 2003, the African Union Mission in Burundi deployed troops to serve as a stabilizing force through disarmament and the postconflict phase.

[a] Paul Nugent, *Africa Since Independence: A Comparative History*, New York: Palgrave Macmillan, 2004, p. 58.

tional multiparty government. He also played a key role in the acceptance of the insurgents as legitimate negotiating partners. As a former revolutionary turned statesman, South Africa's former leader pushed for the involvement of the rebels in talks.[76] The government and the FDD—with its political wing, the National Council for the Defense of Democracy—signed the Protocol on Political Power-Sharing, Defence and Security in Pretoria in October 2003.

Solidifying the peace after this brutal, decade-long civil war was the third-party presence of the African Union Mission in Burundi, which performed admirably in the yearlong transition to a more robust UN force. The African Union mission was composed of one strengthened company of approximately 280 soldiers from Mozambique; one battalion, plus two additional companies (980 soldiers) from Ethiopia; and one battalion complemented by two additional companies (1,600 soldiers) from South Africa, which served as the mission's lead nation.[77]

Chechnya I, 1994–1996

Table 14 describes the steps to settlement in the 1994–1996 Chechen conflict in the context of the master narrative. Despite being heavily outgunned by the Russians, Chechen guerrillas managed to fight the Red Army's successor to a stalemate. Strategically scattered throughout the Chechnya's diverse terrain and organized into platoons of 15–25 fighters, the insurgents were armed with heavy-caliber machine guns and rocket-propelled grenades.[78] The insurgents also enjoyed an internal sanctuary by escaping into the mountains and forests to rest, recuperate, and rearm. Though separate from the fighting against Russian military and paramilitary forces, the guerrillas also perpetrated spectacular terrorist attacks in the heart of Russia. As a demonstration of potency, they executed large-scale hostage-taking operations

---

[76] Filip Reyntjens, "Briefing: Burundi: A Peaceful Transition After a Decade of War?" *African Affairs*, Vol. 105, No. 418, January 2006, p. 118.

[77] Henri Boshoff and Dara Francis, "The AU Mission in Burundi: Technical and Operational Dimensions," *African Security Review*, Vol. 12, No. 3, 2003, p. 41.

[78] Richard H. Shultz, Jr., and Andrea Dew, *Insurgents, Terrorists, and Militias: The Warriors of Contemporary Combat*, New York: Columbia University Press, 2006, p. 124.

Table 14
Chechnya I, 1994–1996 (Outcome: Mixed, Favoring Insurgents)

Step	Narrative
1	By February 1995, Russian forces in Chechnya reached 30,000, including an elite airborne division, naval infantry, and Spetsnaz (special forces) troops.[a] A stalemate ensued, with Chechen guerrillas turning Grozny into an urban battleground.
2	After nearly two years of brutal fighting, during which Russian COIN forces suffered heavy casualties, the head of Russia's Security Council, Alexander Lebed, reached out to Chechen President Aslan Maskhadov in an attempt to quell the violence.
3	Lebed and Maskhadov came to terms on a temporary cease-fire.
4	In August 1996, the COIN force and the insurgents agreed to the Khasavyurt Accord.[b] This agreement focused on the technical aspects of demilitarization, the withdrawal of both sides' forces from Grozny, the creation of a joint headquarters to prevent looting in the city, and a stipulation that any agreement on relations between the Chechen Republic of Ichkeria and the Russian federal government need not be signed until late 2001.
5	After the signing of the Khasavyurt Accord, the Chechens enjoyed de facto independence for about three years, until the Second Chechen War began in August 1999.

[a] Olga Oliker, *Russia's Chechen Wars 1994–2000: Lessons from Urban Combat*, Santa Monica, Calif.: RAND Corporation, MR-1289-A, 2001, p. 23.

[b] Mark Kramer, "The Perils of Counterinsurgency: Russia's War in Chechnya," *International Security*, Vol. 29, No. 3, Winter 2004–2005.

at Budyonnovsk and Pervomayskoye, which drew prominent media attention and struck severe psychological blows to the Russian public.[79]

After being routed by Russian forces on the open plains, the insurgents reentered Grozny in March 1996 and laid siege to the city for three days. In early August 1996, with Russian and Chechen officials in the midst of negotiations to end the conflict, Shamil Basayev led a force of roughly 600 insurgents into Grozny. (Including reinforcements, the insurgent force numbered around 4,000 fighters.)[80] Fight-

---

[79] Robert M. Cassidy, *Russia in Afghanistan and Chechnya: Military Strategic Culture and the Paradoxes of Asymmetric Conflict*, Carlisle, Pa.: Strategic Studies Institute, U.S. Army War College, February 2003, pp. 31–32.

[80] Oliker, 2001, p. 30.

ing raged between Basayev's fighters and Russian internal forces for two weeks in what would be the last battle of the First Chechen War. Russian casualties included 500 dead and another 1,400 wounded or unaccounted for.[81] Russian General Alexander Lebed was tasked with bringing the conflict to an end, and he eventually negotiated a cease-fire with the insurgent leadership. The last two brigades of Russian troops were ordered out in November 1996. The negotiated settlement ultimately collapsed, however, and the Second Chechen War began in 1999.

Democratic Republic of the Congo (Anti-Kabila), 1998–2003

Table 15 shows the narrative progression followed in the Democratic Republic of the Congo (DRC) as the government and insurgents moved toward a settlement that ultimately favored the latter.

Following the assassination of Laurent Kabila by one of his soldiers in early 2001, the deposed leader's son, Joseph, assumed the presidency of the DRC. Known as a more moderate politician than his father, Joseph Kabila demonstrated a much greater interest in political compromise from the very beginning of his tenure. Early on, the younger Kabila initiated international negotiations and worked assiduously to bring the warring parties to the negotiating table. This shift toward more moderate leadership was coupled with changing regional conditions. In neighboring Burundi, the government in Bujumbura worked toward a power-sharing agreement with the FDD. The Burundian government agreed to withdraw its soldiers from the DRC in return for a pledge from Kinshasa to stop supporting FDD insurgents. While fighting continued, this quid pro quo helped map out a path for continued progress toward a settlement.

What became known as the Inter-Congolese Dialogue was far from perfect. However, the long road to a negotiated settlement did include several achievements, such as the Global and Inclusive Agreement on Transition in the Democratic Republic of Congo, which provided for a transitional political arrangement recognizing the existing presidency and allocating four vice-presidential posts to the three major

---

[81] Oliker, 2001, p. 31.

Table 15
Congo (Anti-Kabila), 1998–2003 (Outcome: Mixed, Favoring Insurgents)

Step	Narrative
1	As invading forces from Rwanda and Uganda fought to depose Laurent Kabila, the Congolese leader enlisted Angolan, Zimbabwean, and Namibian troops to aid local militia groups in his defense. Both sides quickly reached a stalemate as the local war morphed into a regional conflict.[a]
2	In July 1999, the Congolese government, numerous regional countries, and several main rebel groups (including the Movement for the Liberation of the Congo and the Rally for Congolese Democracy) signed the Lusaka Accord.[b] Although it fell short in its primary objective of ending the conflict, this official intermediate agreement contained several important provisions, such as a national dialogue between the belligerents, known as the Inter-Congolese Dialogue.
3	The Lusaka Accord called for a cease-fire by all signatories and the withdrawal of foreign forces in a quid pro quo for disarming Hutu militias.[c] The decision to disarm the militias led Rwanda, an important external actor, to take a more conciliatory approach toward the situation in the DRC.
4	After the Lusaka Accord was signed in 1999, subsequent agreements followed, and the Congolese leadership begrudgingly accepted the opposition forces as legitimate negotiating partners. In April 2002, the Sun City Agreement was signed, providing a framework for future elections.
5	In early 2001, Laurent Kabila was assassinated by one of his soldiers and succeeded by his son, Joseph. The younger Kabila fashioned himself as a moderate and favored resolving the conflict through political negotiations rather than on the battlefield.[d]
6	Toward the end of 2002, the Congolese government agreed to a power-sharing deal with the Movement for the Liberation of the Congo and the Rally for Congolese Democracy. An interim government was established in July 2003, leading to the formation of a transitional government.[e]
7	A third-party guarantor in the form of the UN Organization Mission in the Democratic Republic of the Congo helped facilitate elections and the approval of a new constitution in July 2006.

[a] David E. Cunningham, "Veto Players and Civil War Duration," *American Journal of Political Science*, Vol. 50, No. 4, October 2006.

[b] Lusaka Accord of 1999, July 10, 1999.

[c] Rene LeMarchand, "Consociationalism and Power Sharing in Africa: Rwanda, Burundi, and the Democratic Republic of Congo," *African Affairs*, Vol. 106, No. 422, January 2007.

[d] Séverine Autesserre, "The Trouble with Congo: How Local Disputes Fuel Regional Conflict," *Foreign Affairs*, May–June 2008. Although it was not the peace process itself that led to the ascension of the younger Kabila, negotiation was responsible for keeping him in power and in moving the process forward along to steps 6 and 7.

[e] Denis M. Tull and Andreas Mehler, "The Hidden Costs of Power-Sharing: Reproducing Insurgent Violence in Africa," *African Affairs*, Vol. 104, No. 416, July 2005.

armed groups and the unarmed political opposition. Throughout the peace process, the international community played an indispensable role, and the Office of the UN Secretary-General dispatched a special envoy to help facilitate agreement at each step of the process.[82]

Following the Master Narrative Toward an End Game in Afghanistan

With the announcement of a drawdown of troops starting in 2014, the Obama administration has begun to concentrate its efforts on devising an end-game strategy for Afghanistan. According to Sean Maloney, "It is possible that successful negotiations with Mullah Omar's Taliban faction would have some effect, but we must confront the possibility that that window of opportunity is now closed and that we are up against something new."[83] Negotiating with the Taliban is no longer unthinkable, as it might have been a decade ago, but it now seems one of a few likely scenarios for bringing the war in Afghanistan to an end and establishing a modicum of stability after the withdrawal of international troops from a country perpetually in conflict.

To reach a negotiated settlement, it helps if both sides have faced setbacks, neither side perceives unambiguous military victory as likely, external actors reduce support to both sides, and all external actors press for a negotiated settlement (and if at least one is willing to act as a guarantor). Based on these criteria, prospects for a negotiated settlement in Afghanistan look reasonably good if the insurgents are unable to prevail militarily once the coalition withdraws, if insurgents' external supporters push for a negotiated settlement, and if a third party can be found to act as an honest broker and provide peacekeepers.

Our master narrative for reaching a negotiated settlement as applied to Afghanistan suggests that efforts are necessary to make

---

[82] Henri Boshoff and Martin Rupiya, "Delegates, Dialogue, and Desperadoes: The ICD and the DRC Peace Process," *African Security Review*, Vol. 12, No. 3, 2003, p. 31.

[83] Sean M. Maloney, "Can We Negotiate with the Taliban?" *Small Wars and Insurgencies*, Vol. 21, No. 2, June 2012, p. 408.

progress toward steps 2–4. By most accounts, a military stalemate has largely been reached, though this delicate balance may shift considerably following an international withdrawal. According to Thomas Ruttig, "Despite the significant number of casualties the Taliban have suffered, including among commanders, there is no sign that their momentum has been stopped, in spite of U.S. military assertions to the contrary. Instead, their geographic reach, ethnic inclusiveness, and potential for intimidation seem to be growing."[84] The decision by the Obama administration to go ahead with the troop surge and increased drone strikes across the border in Pakistan was supposed to be the great equalizer. However, these changes have not been sufficient to crush the Taliban in the manner that many expected.

With step 1 achieved, the next move in the master narrative is to co-opt the leadership on both sides and put sufficient pressure on respective parties (the United States on the Karzai government, Pakistan on the Taliban) to accept each other as legitimate negotiation participants. This assumes, of course, that both the United States and Pakistan are amenable to a negotiated settlement. Pakistan continues to provide safe haven to Taliban leaders and has undermined attempts to broker a negotiated settlement in Afghanistan in the past. However, the Taliban opened an office in Qatar with the tacit approval of Islamabad. Furthermore, the prospects for peace would be heightened if "first-ring actors," including Iran, Russia, and India, agreed to support peace rather than continued fighting.[85] At some point, there has to be the promise of political legitimacy for the insurgent leadership—as a starting point, not as a measure of last resort.

Step 2: Acceptance of Insurgents as Legitimate Negotiating Partners

To a certain extent, this second step has already happened. Afghan President Hamid Karzai has correctly recognized that the Taliban represent a sizable and local constituency in Afghanistan and thus cannot

---

[84] Thomas Ruttig, *The Battle for Afghanistan: Negotiations with the Taliban*, Washington, D.C.: New America Foundation, May 2011, p. 4. At the time of that book's publication, the troop surge in Afghanistan was just getting under way.

[85] The main actors and groupings appear in Shinn and Dobbins, 2011.

be ignored. With the opening of the Taliban political office in Qatar, the Afghan government and the insurgents are inching closer to actual negotiations.[86] The United States must work assiduously to ensure that whoever succeeds Karzai also accepts the insurgents as legitimate negotiating partners, thus ensuring continuity throughout the process.

Previous attempts by all parties involved to resolve the conflict will likely influence the manner in which future negotiations unfold. In the first few months following the U.S.-led invasion of Afghanistan, scores of Taliban fighters defected for money and promises of honorable positions in a new government. In December 2001, Mullah Omar made a public offering to surrender Kandahar to Afghan tribal leaders.[87] The emir dispatched a group of senior Taliban leaders—Tayyab Agha, Mullah Baradar, Mullah Obaidullah, and Mullah Abdul Razzaq—to negotiate the terms of a surrender.[88] But in December 2001, the United States and the Northern Alliance were not interested in compromise, and they summarily rejected the Taliban's offer (after the Taliban had first rejected the U.S. offer of negotiations immediately following the attacks of September 11, 2001). Ruttig describes the U.S. strategy during this period as "mopping up 'Taliban remnants,'" which served as a complement to its "we do not talk to terrorists" doctrine.[89] Other attempts to resolve the conflict occurred with the reestablishment of the political party Jamiat-e-Khuddam ul-Furqan in late 2001, the Emergency Loya Jirga in 2002, the Saudi Initiative in 2007–2008, the Hezb-e-Islami Gulbuddin (HIG) faction's rapprochement in late 2008, and meetings in Dubai in the spring of 2009, as well as other failed reconciliation initiatives from 2004 to the present.[90]

---

[86] Rod Nordland and Alissa J. Rubin, "Taliban's Divided Tactics Raise Doubts Over Talks," *New York Times*, June 25, 2013.

[87] Omar's public declaration led to the defection of senior Taliban commander Abdul Wahid three years later. Other high-ranking Taliban leaders who have switched sides include the Hotak brothers of Wardak Province, Nur Ali Haidery Ishaqzai, Abdul Salam Rocketi, and the recently assassinated Arsala Rahmani. See Christia and Semple, 2009, p. 36.

[88] Ruttig, 2011, p. 6.

[89] Ruttig, 2011, p. 7.

[90] Ruttig, 2011, pp. 7–8.

Of course, the situation in Afghanistan is complicated by the country's tumultuous history of nearly three straight decades of conflict. Though as Bosnia, Burundi, and Indonesia demonstrate, neither the duration nor the character of a conflict makes it unresolvable. If the government truly accepts the insurgents as legitimate negotiating partners, it can help propel the process forward.

In effect, the task of making sure the Afghan government truly accepts the Taliban as a legitimate negotiating entity is made more difficult by the sheer number of stakeholders, each with varied interests. As Vanda Felbab-Brown rightly points out, "Many Afghan groups fear that a negotiated outcome would be detrimental to their interests and jeopardize their security."[91] These groups include non-Pashtun ethnic groups, such as Tajiks, Uzbeks, and Hazaras, as well as Pashtun subgroups like Kandahari Durrani elites, who compete with Ghilzai Pashtuns for power and influence. More importantly, when a government is fighting multiple insurgent groups simultaneously, as the Philippines case shows, there may be a tendency to paint all insurgent groups with a broad brush, wherein the true goals or objectives of some of these groups may be more reasonable or acceptable to the COIN force than the goals of other, more radical groups.

Step 3: Brokered Cease-Fires

Kabul's current policy of "fight and talk" appears to be the correct one at this point in the conflict. Until the Taliban formally agrees to a cease-fire and engages in serious talks to end the insurgency, ISAF must continue to kill and capture insurgents while also training and equipping the ANSF. Offensive military actions *must* be part of any comprehensive plan. Offensive power must serve as a complement to diplomacy and politics.

While spoilers can threaten a peace process politically, splinter groups can emerge to threaten the process—and any resulting stability—militarily. Even "small elements of 'irredeemables'" can cause major problems for a country in transition from war to peace. Often,

---

[91] Vanda Felbab-Brown, "Afghanistan in 2012: Limited Progress and Threatening Future," *Asian Survey*, Vol. 53, No. 1, January–February 2013, p. 27.

because they are smaller and may be desperate, splinter groups resort to extremely violent and sometimes indiscriminate attacks.[92] Just as with spoilers, the success or failure of negotiations can hinge on whether or not policymakers are able to devise a plan to deal with splinters before the latter undertake a concerted effort to destabilize a negotiated settlement.[93] Where external actors can influence a cease-fire, as in the DRC, the COIN force must seek to leverage and exploit every possible avenue in arriving at this third step in the process.

To bring an end to the insurgency, Taliban fighters must be reintegrated into Afghan society and their representatives included in any future government.[94] Before reintegration can take place in earnest, there must be some form of cease-fire.[95] As James Shinn and James Dobbins have pointed out, a cease-fire could provide the space for a more comprehensive accord or an official intermediate agreement, especially if this agreement were preceded by other confidence-building measures (e.g., prisoner releases, a guarantee of safe passage for negotiations).[96] Exactly how, and under what circumstances, insurgents make the transition to ex-combatants holds far-reaching implications for the stability of the Afghan state and the likelihood of continued violence following the withdrawal of foreign troops. Determining the right balance between withdrawing U.S. troops and maintaining enough of a presence to deal with residual security issues and training of ANSF personnel could be a major sticking point in any negotiated settlement. Furthermore, it remains to be seen whether the Taliban is willing to integrate into an Afghan government with a dominant non-Pashtun element.

---

[92] Ben Connable and Martin Libicki, *How Insurgencies End*, Santa Monica, Calif.: RAND Corporation, MG-965-MCIA, 2010, p. 154.

[93] Audrey Kurth Cronin, *When Should We Talk to Terrorists?* Washington, D.C.: United States Institute of Peace, Special Report No. 240, May 2010, p. 1.

[94] Karen DeYoung, Peter Finn, and Craig Whitlock, "Taliban in Talks with Karzai Government," *Washington Post*, October 6, 2010.

[95] Kenneth Katzman, *Afghanistan: Post-Taliban Governance, Security, and U.S. Policy*, Washington, D.C.: Congressional Research Service, June 25, 2013, p. 40.

[96] The main actors and groupings appear in Shinn and Dobbins, 2011, p. 82.

Step 4: Official Intermediate Agreements

On a more micro-level, reintegration efforts in Afghanistan have proceeded on and off since 2001. Unlike macro-level reconciliation efforts, which include high-level strategic and political dialogue, *reintegration* refers to tactical and operational efforts to assimilate low- and mid-ranking fighters back into their local villages and provinces.[97] Since 2010, the locus of reintegration efforts has been the Afghan Peace and Reintegration Program (APRP), which is "based on a broad strategic vision led by Afghan men and women for a peaceful, stable and prosperous Afghanistan."[98] Intermediate agreements are most likely through the APRP. The program's implementation is proceeding on two tracks. The first track centers on reintegrating low- and mid-level fighters back into their local communities (the "operational level"), while the second track is geared toward reconciling with members of the insurgent leadership to permit them back into Afghan society (the "strategic and political levels").[99]

Negotiating with the leadership is paramount, but having a plan in place to deal with mid-tier commanders ("tier 2") of the insurgency is essential. If the Taliban leadership brokers a deal to end the fighting, those insurgents on the battlefield will need a respectable exit strategy. Insurgents, as stakeholders, are guardians of specific interests. Therefore, fighters are more likely to accept the role of ex-combatant if they perceive that the benefits of doing so outweigh the costs. A well-organized reintegration program would offer these individuals the benefits of comradeship, security, livelihood, and respectability.[100] Part of a successful reintegration program will be recognizing the diversity of the insurgency and tailoring reintegration packages to the insurgents. While cash payments may work for some, they may not work for others. To this end, the United States needs to study lessons learned

---

[97] Seth G. Jones, *Reintegrating Afghan Insurgents*, Santa Monica, Calif.: RAND Corporation, OP-327-MCIA, 2011a, p. ix.

[98] Islamic Republic of Afghanistan National Security Council, *Afghanistan Peace and Reintegration Program (APRP) Programme*, project document, July 2010, p. 1.

[99] We thank Jason Campbell at RAND for this observation.

[100] Christia and Semple, 2009, p. 41.

from previous demobilization, disarmament, and reintegration programs to discern what has worked and what has been less successful.

Step 5: Power-Sharing Offers

Despite the proliferation of recent studies calling for a negotiated peace in Afghanistan, history tells us that while success may require negotiation, negotiations in and of themselves do not equal success.[101] In his analysis of negotiating with insurgent groups, Daniel Byman points out several of the dangers inherent in inviting a group like the Taliban into a power-sharing arrangement.[102] Because of their organizational skills, propensity to intimidate locals and genuine popularity in parts of the country, there is a possibility that the Taliban could be victorious in future elections.

As unappealing as it may be to offer insurgents a place in the government, a power-sharing deal is a necessary step to bringing the conflict to an end. That said, moving from step 4 to step 5 can take time. In Burundi, it took a while before the incumbents could seriously consider sharing power with the insurgents. "Allowing insurgents into the political process can be an important tool for accommodating the insurgency's cause, holding them accountable to their constituents, and bringing them under the legal strictures of the state."[103] When Martin McGuinness, Hassan Nasrallah, and Nelson Mandela were first afforded political legitimacy, there were certainly many observers who harbored strong doubt about the wisdom of such a move. However, each insurgent-turned-politician did an admirable job of making the transition, with some exceptions (particularly in Nasrallah's case). As Steve Coll notes, "The lures of legitimacy and political influence

---

[101] Among some of the most important studies on a possible negotiated peace in Afghanistan are Matt Waldman, *Dangerous Liaisons with the Afghan Taliban: The Feasibility and Risks of Negotiation*, Washington, D.C.: United States Institute of Peace, Special Report No. 256, October 2010; Ruttig, 2011; and Michael Semple, *Reconciliation in Afghanistan*, Washington, D.C.: United States Institute of Peace, 2009.

[102] Daniel Byman, 2009, p. 136. As defined in this report, power-sharing need not include a guarantee of state resources but merely the opportunity to compete for power.

[103] Heather S. Gregg, "Setting a Place at the Table: Ending Insurgencies Through the Political Process," *Small Wars and Insurgencies*, Vol. 22, No. 4, October 2011, p. 660.

may eventually tempt others in the Taliban's aging leadership."[104] To the extent that legitimacy and popular recognition are a conferral of enhanced status to former political pariahs like the Taliban, this is a necessary evil in the negotiation process.[105] This is now an official part of British strategy, as outlined in a 2009 policy paper that noted "the importance of offering a route back into mainstream politics and society for insurgents willing to renounce violence and embrace the Afghan constitution."[106]

Group behavior is typically an indicator of intentions. Some insurgents are undoubtedly motivated by a strict adherence to Islam, which is used to mobilize the group.[107] Would the Taliban seriously consider a power-sharing government, or would the group use negotiations to win prisoner releases, buy time, and then storm back to take power once international forces left Afghanistan? After relying more on narcotics to fund their fight, have the insurgents made a transformation similar to the Revolutionary Armed Forces of Colombia (FARC), in which entire elements of the organization are more interested in profit than politics? Some research suggests that as insurgent groups become more intimately involved with the drug trade, their ideological commitment is enervated in direct relation to an increased interest in purely economic ends.[108] But this is not always true. The PIRA in Northern Ireland, the Kurdistan Workers' Party (PKK), and the Liberation Tigers of Tamil Eelam (LTTE) in Sri Lanka each engaged in forms of organized crime without deviating from their true role as insurgents.[109] To determine

---

[104] Steve Coll, "Looking for Mullah Omar," *New Yorker*, Vol. 87, No. 45, January 23, 2012.

[105] Weinberg, Pedahzur, and Perliger, *Political Parties and Terrorist Groups*, London: Routledge, 2009, p. 144.

[106] Her Majesty's Government, *UK Policy in Afghanistan and Pakistan: The Way Forward*, London, 2009, p. 8.

[107] Seth G. Jones, "The Rise of Afghanistan's Insurgency: State Failure and Jihad," *International Security*, Vol. 32, No. 4, Spring 2008.

[108] Svante Cornell, "Narcotics and Armed Conflict: Interaction and Implications," *Studies in Conflict and Terrorism*, Vol. 30, No. 3, 2007, p. 208.

[109] The PIRA, PKK, and LTTE are not among what Thomas Mockaitis labels "degenerate insurgencies," which are insurgent movements that degenerate into mere extremist orga-

whether the Taliban are insurgents or criminals requires analysis of the group's *raison d'etre*. Extensive field research conducted by Sultan Barakat and Steven Zyck suggests that the Taliban's motives are more parochial than usually assumed—and related to traditional Pashtun norms, such as revenge and respect.[110] Relying on its vast trove of data on Taliban members, the United States can leverage its superior intelligence capabilities—as the British did in Northern Ireland—to parse smugglers from statesmen, though in Afghanistan, these two positions are not necessarily mutually exclusive.

Step 6: Moderation in Leadership

Karzai's public statements occasionally refer to the Taliban as "sons of the soil" in an effort to convince the world that the group is a fact of life when envisioning the future of Afghanistan. If it is true that, as some suggest, Mullah Omar is surrounded by pragmatists who are open to compromise with the West and crave political legitimacy, this bodes well for a negotiated settlement. But there are also many ideologues within the group who are certain to cause a rift within the organization as negotiations gain traction.[111]

Splintering and spoiling both remain acute possibilities with respect to a negotiated settlement. Like most insurgent groups, the Taliban has its share of hardcore fighters who will refuse to give up

---

nizations capable of conducting little more than terrorist attacks (Basque Homeland and Freedom [ETA]) or morphing into criminal organizations (FARC, Sendero Luminoso). See Thomas R. Mockaitis, *Resolving Insurgencies*, Carlisle, Pa.: Strategic Studies Institute, U.S. Army War College, June 2011, pp. 37–48. Both Makarenko's "model of terrorist-criminal relationships" and Cornell's "crime-rebellion nexus" suggest that the relationship between insurgency and organized crime should not be conceived of in terms of path analysis but, rather, as a sliding scale on which groups can go back and forth between the extremes of crime and ideological insurgency, occupying any number of intermediate stages between these poles along the way. See Tamara Makarenko, "The Crime-Terror Continuum: Tracing the Interplay Between Transnational Organized Crime and Terrorism," *Global Crime*, Vol. 6, No. 1, February 2004, and Cornell, 2007.

[110] Sultan Barakat and Steven A. Zyck, "Afghanistan's Insurgency and the Viability of a Political Settlement," *Studies in Conflict and Terrorism*, Vol. 33, No. 3, 2010, pp. 196–198.

[111] Jayshree Bajoria and Zachary Laub, *Backgrounder: The Taliban in Afghanistan*, New York: Council on Foreign Relations, August 6, 2013.

the fight, especially those who see it as a religious obligation to retake the country and implement *sharia* in an Islamic emirate governed by religious leaders. The extent to which the Taliban's ideology will affect possible negotiations is a question of much speculation. The Taliban has already moderated its position on several fronts. This moderation is largely superficial and is mostly an attempt to avoid alienating potential supporters in its quest for legitimacy. If negotiations do take place, ideological hardliners could seek to play the role of spoiler, as they did in the post-Bonn period.[112] To that end, radical splinter groups aligned with the Haqqani Network or al-Qaeda remnants are almost guaranteed to emerge following a negotiated settlement.

With regard to spoilers—leaders and parties whose power, worldview, or interests are threatened by peace negotiations—a preemptive strategy to deal with their emergence can help mitigate negative outcomes.[113] As Christia and Semple have observed, "Some leaders and commanders who are influential within the movement are open to rapprochement, but a dialogue conducted through a single authorized channel could be hijacked by Taliban hard-liners."[114] If not handled properly, spoilers have the ability to sabotage the entire peace process. In Afghanistan, potential spoiler groups abound, including HIG, the Haqqani Network, and Pakistan's Inter-Services Intelligence. For the United States to craft the correct policy intervention, policymakers must correctly diagnose the intentions and motivations of the spoilers.[115] Groups not amenable to compromise must be sidelined or eliminated.

In their *International Security* article, "Let Us Now Praise Great Men," Daniel Byman and Kenneth Pollack lament the tendency of

---

[112] Mohammad Masoom Stanekzai, *Thwarting Afghanistan's Insurgency: A Pragmatic Approach Toward Peace and Reconciliation*, Washington, D.C.: United States Institute of Peace, September 2008, pp. 9–10.

[113] Alex Braithwaite, Dennis M. Foster, and David A. Sobek, "Ballots, Bargains, and Bombs: Terrorist Targeting of Spoiler Opportunities," *International Interactions*, Vol. 36, No. 3, 2010.

[114] Christia and Semple, 2009, p. 40.

[115] Stedman, 1997.

political scientists to downplay the role of individuals in international relations. Indeed, as the authors note, attempting to understand international relations while ignoring Hitler, Bismarck, or Napoleon "is like trying to understand art or music without Michelangelo or Mozart."[116] In Afghanistan, there is an ongoing debate over exactly how much power Mullah Omar still wields over the insurgency. Steve Coll's *New Yorker* essay "Looking for Mullah Omar" includes quotes from several individuals closely connected to the Obama administration's Afghanistan-Pakistan (AFPAK) policy. Vali Nasr, a professor of international politics at Tufts University and former U.S. State Department official, said the following of Mullah Omar: "Both symbolically and pragmatically, [Omar] held all the keys to unlocking the Taliban problem. There is no legitimacy to a Taliban decision without him. . . . He is the Ho Chi Minh of the war."[117] Coll also reports an unnamed former senior Obama administration figure as stating, "I've come to the conclusion that Mullah Omar is still the big boss. All threads still lead back to him." Finally, the late Richard Holbrooke, who served as U.S. Special Envoy for Afghanistan and Pakistan related, "I think Mullah Omar is incredibly important. The more I look at this thing, the more I think he is a driving, inspirational force whose capture or elimination would have a material effect."[118]

Seducing the moderate elements of the insurgency requires, first, identifying them. This step alone can pose a serious barrier to success and sometimes, as in the DRC or in the Philippines, moderate leadership follows on the heels of a previously unforeseen or unpredictable event, like an assassination or military coup (as in those two conflicts). Some have claimed that there is a sharp distinction between "doves" and "hawks" within the Taliban's ranks, the former represented by individuals like Mullah Abdul Ghani Baradar and the latter represented

---

[116] Daniel Byman and Kenneth M. Pollack, "Let Us Now Praise Great Men: Bringing the Statesman Back In," *International Security*, Vol. 25, No. 4, Spring 2001, p. 145.

[117] Steve Coll, "Looking for Mullah Omar," *The New Yorker*, Vol. 87, No. 45, January 23, 2012.

[118] Coll, 2012.

by Mullah Omar himself.[119] The internal divide within the Taliban is between those who are pushing for talks and those who steadfastly resist negotiations.[120]

Step 7: Third-Party Guarantors

A comprehensive COIN strategy must include aspects of military power and economic power, but also critical elements of what Joseph Nye, Jr., calls "soft power." U.S. government policies of public diplomacy, as along with bilateral and multilateral diplomacy, are the cornerstone of soft-power efforts to settle the war through negotiation.[121]

Just as President Obama ordered a surge of troops to fight Taliban insurgents, the United States and its allies must unleash a diplomatic surge of equal if not greater intensity. This diplomatic surge would target the countries with the most influence in Afghanistan, the most important of which is Pakistan. Other countries at the forefront of this diplomatic surge would be such "first-ring" actors as India, Iran, and Russia, followed by "second-ring" actors, including Turkey, Saudi Arabia, China, and European leadership. Finally, it may be worthwhile to consider lesser but still affected regional actors, such as Turkmenistan, Tajikistan, and Uzbekistan.[122]

Negotiating with the Taliban leadership raises the question of the role of outside actors in official peace talks. As a major player in the conflict over the past decade, the United States is unlikely to be accepted as a neutral third party, compromising its ability to guarantee talks and a settlement. Ideally, some other third-party guarantor would be found. Perhaps the UN or one or more other national actors (countries that have been mentioned in discussions include Turkey, Qatar,

---

[119] John Bew, Ryan Evans, Martyn Frampton, Peter Neumann, and Marisa Porges, *Talking to the Taliban: Hope Over History?* London: International Centre for the Study of Radicalisation, King's College London, 2013, p. 29.

[120] Hasan Kahn, "To Talk or Not To Talk: The Taliban's Internal Divide," *Foreign Policy*, December 10, 2009.

[121] Joseph S. Nye, Jr., *Soft Power: The Means to Success in World Politics*, New York: PublicAffairs, 2004, p. 31.

[122] The main actors and groupings appear in Shinn and Dobbins, 2011.

and Saudi Arabia) can play this role.[123] If a new third party becomes heavily invested in the peace process, the success of step 7 becomes more likely, but the United States will be forced to accept less control over negotiations.

As mentioned earlier in this report, any negotiated settlement will likely be "mixed." It is possible that the Afghan government, the Taliban, and the United States and coalition forces will all have to make concessions to reach an agreement. If this happens, Afghanistan may have to accept former insurgents into its government, the Taliban could be asked to unequivocally renounce any and all ties with al-Qaeda, and the United States and its coalition partners would face the difficult decision of whether to follow through on current plans to significantly reduce their presence, perhaps even withdrawing all forces from Afghanistan. The release of Taliban prisoners in Guantanamo could be a confidence-building measure used to jump-start the negotiation process. Other issues, such as women's rights, narcotics, and the disarmament of militias, could potentially be shelved for discussion at a later date.

Conclusion

In January 2012, then–Secretary of Defense Leon Panetta outlined the most pressing threats facing the United States—terrorism, Iran, North Korea, nuclear proliferation, cyberwar, and the threat of a rising China.[124] He also noted that, before the United States can turn its full attention to these threats, it needs to resolve the smoldering insurgency in Afghanistan. Of the major insurgent groups opposing the Afghan government, none is more important than the Afghan Taliban.[125] The

---

[123]Because the UN is not an autonomous actor, several countries will have to step up to dominate the lion's share of resources, further complicating the organization's potential role as a third-party guarantor.

[124]Donna Miles, "Panetta Discusses Defense Issues on '60 Minutes,'" American Forces Press Service, January 30, 2012.

[125]In addition to the Taliban, a panoply of insurgent groups operate in the AFPAK theater, including the Haqqani Network, HIG, Tehrik-i-Taliban, and Lashkar-e-Taiba.

terminal phase of the conflict will entail a shift from the current COIN strategy to a focus on stability operations, including practical end-state objectives within Afghanistan, to include *reconciliation with* and *reintegration of* elements of the insurgency.[126] Pursuing talks with the insurgents and accepting the reconciliation of Taliban members willing to renounce al-Qaeda are necessary steps toward a negotiated cease-fire and political settlement.[127]

Because the Taliban is structured as a horizontal organization, it is not completely clear how much control the Quetta Shura commands over other branches of the organization. If Mullah Omar gives the order to negotiate, who will follow? Anecdotal evidence suggests that a significant rift has been developing between mid-level Taliban commanders and the group's leadership. Many of these mid-level commanders and fighters in the field have expressed a desire to quit the fight.[128] Meanwhile, the Quetta Shura has grown more alienated from realities on the ground, removed from the day-to-day banality of protracted guerrilla warfare. If the Taliban leadership were to negotiate an end to the conflict, it is likely that it would face only sporadic pockets of resistance from foot soldiers in Afghanistan.

The majority of Afghans want peace.[129] Inevitably, the longer the conflict drags on, the more Afghan civilians are killed. Understandably, Afghans are war-weary following more than 30 years of near-constant conflict. If the Taliban is seen as a force for stability in the country, its members may be able to concentrate significant support from the Pashtun population.

Yet, there is reason to be pessimistic. An April 2012 U.S. Department of Defense report to Congress on Afghanistan stated that "the

---

[126]For definitions and major differences between reintegration and reconciliation, see Mark E. Johnson, "Reintegration and Reconciliation in Afghanistan: Time to End the Conflict," *Military Review*, November–December, 2010, p. 97.

[127]Paul D. Miller, "The US and Afghanistan After 2014," *Survival*, Vol. 55, No. 1, February–March 2013, p. 99.

[128]Carlotta Gall, "Midlevel Taliban Admit to a Rift with Top Leaders," *New York Times*, February 21, 2011.

[129]Shinn and Dobbins, 2011, p. 5.

insurgency's safe haven in Pakistan, as well as the limited capacity of the Afghan Government, remains the biggest risk to the process of turning security gains into a durable and sustainable Afghanistan. The insurgency benefits from safe havens inside Pakistan with notable operational and regenerative capacity."[130] The continuing ability of the Taliban to use Pakistan as sanctuary provides it with a clear advantage should the insurgency's goal be to "wait out" the United States before returning to Afghanistan after a U.S. withdrawal and retaking the country by force. At the end of the day, there is little the United States can do militarily to force the Pakistanis to eliminate this safe haven. After all, Pakistan is a long-term partner with six times the population of Iraq, in addition to a growing arsenal of nuclear weapons.[131] Getting Pakistani buy-in on the Taliban is indispensable to success in Afghanistan. According to Seth Jones, "in return for Pakistan's cooperation, the United States could assist the country in putting down the Baluchi independence insurgency, a major thorn in Pakistan's side."[132] This would cost the United States little and might result in a major return on investment if Islamabad followed through on its end of the bargain.

The most important battle of the war is not between ISAF soldiers and Taliban insurgents. Rather, it is the battle for legitimacy between the Afghan government and the Taliban. Mullah Omar's biannual essays emphasize the corruption and injustice of the Karzai administration while attempting to convince the Afghan population that Taliban rule is a better alternative to the past decade of graft and criminality of the "Kabul mafia."

As the United States decreases its military presence in Afghanistan, it will have to rely more on negotiations and less on force to accomplish its mission. A major question for U.S. policymakers is whether the Taliban's decision to open a political office in Qatar means

---

[130] U.S. Department of Defense, *Report on Progress Toward Security and Stability in Afghanistan*, Washington, D.C., April 2012, p. 1.

[131] James F. Dobbins, *After the Taliban: Nation-Building in Afghanistan*, Washington, D.C.: Potomac Books, 2008, p. 166.

[132] Seth G. Jones, "Why the Haqqani Network Is the Wrong Target: To Save Afghanistan, Deal with the Taliban," *Foreign Affairs*, November 6, 2011b.

that the group is serious about negotiations, or whether this act merely signals an attempt to "run down the clock" to the 2014 transition by "dragging out the preliminaries to negotiation."[133] In a recent interview about the pending withdrawal of U.S. troops, journalist Frud Bezhan commented on the United States' lack of leverage in future negotiations: "We're running very short on both carrots and sticks—things we can offer the Taliban and things we can use to intimidate the Taliban into a deal—because we're leaving."[134] Continued support for the Afghan government and for the development of the ANSF can allow the United States to retain some leverage and could improve the negotiating position of the Afghan government. When asked by Bob Woodward what his message was to the people of Afghanistan, President Obama responded, "Our commitment to your long-term security and stability will extend for a very long time, and in the same way that our commitment to Iraq will extend beyond our combat role there. But it's time for us to start thinking in terms of how you guys are going to be able to stand on your own two feet."[135]

When the variables feeding an insurgent organization's strategic decisionmaking apparatus are considered together, negotiations can be considered just as complex as military operations. Because of the number of actors participating, the length of negotiations, and the varying degrees of commitment exhibited by the parties involved, the negotiation process can prove perplexing and even insurmountable to highly capable nations, including the United States.

---

[133] Felbab-Brown, 2013, p. 26.

[134] Frud Bezhan, "Why Is It So Hard to Negotiate with the Taliban?" *The Atlantic*, June 29, 2013.

[135] Bob Woodward, *Obama's Wars*, New York: Simon and Schuster, 2010, p. 375.

References

Adams, Gerry, *Before the Dawn: An Autobiography*, New York: William Morrow and Co., 1996.

Alden, Chris, "The UN and Resolution of Conflict in Mozambique," *Journal of Modern African Studies*, Vol. 33, No. 1, March 1995, pp. 103–128.

Autesserre, Séverine, "The Trouble with Congo: How Local Disputes Fuel Regional Conflict," *Foreign Affairs*, May–June 2008.

Bajoria, Jayshree, and Zachary Laub, *Backgrounder: The Taliban in Afghanistan*, New York: Council on Foreign Relations, August 6, 2013. As of October 4, 2013: http://www.cfr.org/afghanistan/taliban-afghanistan/p10551

Bamford, Bradley W. C., "The Role and Effectiveness of Intelligence in Northern Ireland," *Intelligence and National Security*, Vol. 20, No. 4, December 2005, pp. 581–607.

Barakat, Sultan, and Steven A. Zyck, "Afghanistan's Insurgency and the Viability of a Political Settlement," *Studies in Conflict and Terrorism*, Vol. 33, No. 3, 2010, pp. 193–210.

Barter, Shane Joshua, "Resources, Religion, Rebellion: The Sources and Lessons of Acehnese Separatism," *Small Wars and Insurgencies*, Vol. 19, No. 1, March 2008, pp. 39–61.

Bartole, Andrea, Aldo Civico, and Leone Gianturco, "Mozambique—Renamo," in Bruce W. Drayton and Louis Kriesberg, eds., *Conflict Transformation and Peacebuilding: Moving from Violence to Sustainable Peace*, London: Routledge, 2009, pp. 140–155.

Bell, J. Bowyer, *The Secret Army: The IRA*, rev. 3rd ed., New Brunswick, N.J.: Transaction Publishers, 1997.

Bew, John, Ryan Evans, Martyn Frampton, Peter Neumann, and Marisa Porges, *Talking to the Taliban: Hope Over History?* London: International Centre for the Study of Radicalisation, King's College London, 2013.

Bezhan, Frud, "Why Is It So Hard to Negotiate with the Taliban?" *The Atlantic*, June 29, 2013. As of October 4, 2013:
http://www.theatlantic.com/international/archive/2013/06/why-is-it-so-hard-to-negotiate-with-the-taliban/277353/

Boshoff, Henri, and Dara Francis, "The AU Mission in Burundi: Technical and Operational Dimensions," *African Security Review*, Vol. 12, No. 3, 2003, pp. 41–44.

Boshoff, Henri, and Martin Rupiya, "Delegates, Dialogue, and Desperadoes: The ICD and the DRC Peace Process," *African Security Review*, Vol. 12, No. 3, 2003, pp. 29–37.

Braithwaite, Alex, Dennis M. Foster, and David A. Sobek, "Ballots, Bargains, and Bombs: Terrorist Targeting of Spoiler Opportunities," *International Interactions*, Vol. 36, No. 3, 2010, pp. 294–305.

Byman, Daniel, "Talking with Insurgents: A Guide for the Perplexed," *Washington Quarterly*, Vol. 32, No. 2, April 2009, pp. 125–137.

Byman, Daniel, and Kenneth M. Pollack, "Let Us Now Praise Great Men: Bringing the Statesman Back In," *International Security*, Vol. 25, No. 4, Spring 2001, pp. 107–146.

Cassidy, Robert M., *Russia in Afghanistan and Chechnya: Military Strategic Culture and the Paradoxes of Asymmetric Conflict*, Carlisle, Pa.: Strategic Studies Institute, U.S. Army War College, February 2003.

Centre for International Cooperation and Security, "Disarmament, Demobilisation, and Reintegration (DDR) and Human Security in Cambodia," Bradford, UK: University of Bradford, July 2007.

Chivvis, Christopher S., "The Dayton Dilemma," *Survival*, Vol. 52, No. 5, October–November 2010, pp. 47–74.

Christia, Fotini, and Michael Semple, "Flipping the Taliban: How to Win in Afghanistan," *Foreign Affairs*, July–August 2009, pp. 34–45.

Clarke, Colin, *Throwing in the Towel: Why Insurgents Negotiate*, doctoral dissertation, Pittsburgh, Pa.: University of Pittsburgh, January 2013.

Coll, Steve, "Looking for Mullah Omar," *New Yorker*, Vol. 87, No. 45, January 23, 2012.

Connable, Ben, and Martin Libicki, *How Insurgencies End*, Santa Monica, Calif.: RAND Corporation, MG-965-MCIA, 2010. As of October 4, 2013:
http://www.rand.org/pubs/monographs/MG965.html

Coogan, Tim Pat, *The IRA*, New York: Palgrave, 2000.

Cornell, Svante, "Narcotics and Armed Conflict: Interaction and Implications," *Studies in Conflict and Terrorism*, Vol. 30, No. 3, 2007, pp. 207–227.

Cronin, Audrey Kurth, "How al-Qaida Ends: The Decline and Demise of Terrorist Groups," in Robert J. Art and Kenneth Waltz, eds., *The Use of Force: Military Power and International Politics*, Lanham, Md.: Rowman and Littlefield, 2009.

———, *When Should We Talk to Terrorists?* Washington, D.C.: United States Institute of Peace, Special Report No. 240, May 2010.

Cunningham, David E., "Veto Players and Civil War Duration," *American Journal of Political Science*, Vol. 50, No. 4, October 2006, pp. 875–892.

Dadmehr, Nasrin, "Tajikistan: Regionalism and Weakness," in Robert I. Rotberg, ed., *State Failure and State Weakness in a Time of Terror*, Washington, D.C.: Brookings Institution Press, 2003, pp. 245–264.

DeYoung, Karen, Peter Finn, and Craig Whitlock, "Taliban in Talks with Karzai Government," *Washington Post*, October 6, 2010. As of October 4, 2013: http://www.washingtonpost.com/wp-dyn/content/article/2010/10/05/AR2010100506636.html

Dobbins, James F., *After the Taliban: Nation-Building in Afghanistan*, Washington, D.C.: Potomac Books, 2008.

Dobbins, James, John G. McGinn, Keith Crane, Seth G. Jones, Rollie Lal, Andrew Rathmell, Rachel M. Swanger, and Anga R. Timilsina, *America's Role in Nation-Building: From Germany to Iraq*, Santa Monica, Calif.: RAND Corporation, MR-1753-RC, 2003. As of October 4, 2013: http://www.rand.org/pubs/monograph_reports/MR1753.html

Durch, William J., "Building on Sand: UN Peacekeeping in the Western Sahara," *International Security*, Vol. 17, No. 4, Spring 1993, pp. 151–171.

English, Richard, *Armed Struggle: The History of the IRA*, Oxford, UK: Oxford University Press, 2003.

Felbab-Brown, Vanda, "Afghanistan in 2012: Limited Progress and Threatening Future," *Asian Survey*, Vol. 53, No. 1, January–February 2013, pp. 22–33.

Findley, Michael G., "Bargaining and the Interdependent States of Civil War Resolution," *Journal of Conflict Resolution*, Vol. 57, No. 5, October 2013, pp. 905–932.

Fortna, Virginia Page, *Peace Time: Cease-Fire Agreements and the Durability of Peace*, Princeton, N.J.: Princeton University Press, 2004a.

———, "Where Have All the Victories Gone? War Outcomes in Historical Perspective," paper presented at the American Political Science Association annual meeting, Chicago, Ill., September 2, 2004b.

Frampton, Martyn, *The Return of the Militants: Violent Dissident Republicanism*, London: International Centre for the Study of Radicalisation, King's College London, 2010.

Gall, Carlotta, "Midlevel Taliban Admit to a Rift with Top Leaders," *New York Times*, February 21, 2011.

Gleason, Gregory, "The Politics of Counterinsurgency in Central Asia," *Problems of Post-Communism*, Vol. 49, No. 2, March–April 2002, pp. 3–14.

Grandolini, Albert, Tom Cooper, and Troung, "Cambodia, 1954–1999; Part 3," ACIG.org Indochina Database, January 25, 2004. As of October 4, 2013: http://www.acig.org/artman/publish/article_411.shtml

Gregg, Heather S., "Setting a Place at the Table: Ending Insurgencies Through the Political Process," *Small Wars and Insurgencies*, Vol. 22, No. 4, October 2011, pp. 644–668.

Hartzell, Caroline A., "Explaining the Stability of Negotiated Settlements to Intrastate Wars," *Journal of Conflict Resolution*, Vol. 43, No. 1, February 1999, pp. 3–22.

Hartzell, Caroline A., and Matthew Hoddie, *Crafting Peace: Power-Sharing Institutions and the Negotiated Settlement of Civil Wars*, University Park, Pa.: Penn State University Press, 2007.

Her Majesty's Government, *UK Policy in Afghanistan and Pakistan: The Way Forward*, London, 2009.

Horgan, John, and John F. Morrison, "Here to Stay? The Rising Threat of Violent Dissident Republicanism in Northern Ireland," *Terrorism and Political Violence*, Vol. 23, No. 4, 2011, pp. 642–669.

International Crisis Group, *Aceh: A New Chance for Peace*, Asia Briefing No. 40, Jakarta and Brussels, August 15, 2005. As of October 4, 2013: http://www.crisisgroup.org/en/regions/asia/south-east-asia/indonesia/B040-aceh-a-new-chance-for-peace.aspx

———, *Western Sahara: Out of the Impasse*, Middle East/North Africa Report No. 66, Cairo and Brussels, June 11, 2007. As of October 4, 2013: http://www.crisisgroup.org/en/regions/middle-east-north-africa/north-africa/western-sahara/066-western-sahara-out-of-the-impasse.aspx

Islamic Republic of Afghanistan National Security Council, *Afghanistan Peace and Reintegration Program (APRP) Programme,* project document, Kabul, Afghanistan, July 2010. As of October 4, 2013: http://www.undp.org/content/dam/undp/documents/projects/AFG/00060777/00060777_APRP_National%20Programme%20Document%202010%2006%2001.pdf

Joes, Anthony James, *Guerrilla Warfare: A Historical, Biographical, and Bibliographical Sourcebook*, Westport, Conn.: Greenwood Press, 1996.

Johnson, Mark E., "Reintegration and Reconciliation in Afghanistan: Time to End the Conflict," *Military Review*, November–December 2010, pp. 97–101.

Johnston, Patrick, "Negotiated Settlements and Government Strategy in Civil War: Evidence from Darfur," *Civil Wars*, Vol. 9, No. 4, December 2007, pp. 359–377.

Joint Declaration of 15 December 1993 (Downing St. Declaration), 1993. As of August 13, 2013:
http://www.dfa.ie/home/index.aspx?id=8734

Jones, Seth G., "The Rise of Afghanistan's Insurgency: State Failure and Jihad," *International Security*, Vol. 32, No. 4, Spring 2008, pp. 7–40.

———, *Reintegrating Afghan Insurgents*, Santa Monica, Calif.: RAND Corporation, OP-327-MCIA, 2011a. As of October 4, 2013:
http://www.rand.org/pubs/occasional_papers/OP327.html

———, "Why the Haqqani Network Is the Wrong Target: To Save Afghanistan, Deal with the Taliban," *Foreign Affairs*, November 6, 2011b.

Kahn, Hasan, "To Talk or Not To Talk: The Taliban's Internal Divide," *Foreign Policy*, December 10, 2009.

Katzman, Kenneth, *Afghanistan: Post-Taliban Governance, Security, and U.S. Policy*, Washington, D.C.: Congressional Research Service, June 25, 2013.

Koebler, Jason, "Why Governments Should Negotiate with Terrorists," *U.S. News and World Report*, July 31, 2012. As of October 4, 2013:
http://www.usnews.com/news/articles/2012/07/31/
why-governments-should-negotiate-with-terrorists

Kramer, Mark, "The Perils of Counterinsurgency: Russia's War in Chechnya," *International Security*, Vol. 29, No. 3, Winter 2004–2005, pp. 5–63.

Kriesberg, Louis, *Constructive Conflicts: From Escalation to Resolution*, Lanham, Md.: Rowman and Littlefield, 2003.

LeMarchand, Rene, "Consociationalism and Power Sharing in Africa: Rwanda, Burundi, and the Democratic Republic of Congo," *African Affairs*, Vol. 106, No. 422, January 2007, pp. 1–20.

Licklider, Roy, "The Consequences of Negotiated Settlements in Civil Wars, 1945–1993," *American Political Science Review*, Vol. 89, No. 3, September 1995, pp. 681–690.

Lusaka Accord of 1999, July 10, 1999. As of July 26, 2013:
http://www.cfr.org/africa-sub-saharan/lusaka-accord-1999/p23760

Lynch, Dov, "The Tajik Civil War and Peace Process," *Civil Wars*, Vol. 4, No. 4, 2001, pp. 49–72.

Makarenko, Tamara, "The Crime-Terror Continuum: Tracing the Interplay Between Transnational Organized Crime and Terrorism," *Global Crime*, Vol. 6, No. 1, February 2004, pp. 129–145.

Maloney, Sean M., "Can We Negotiate with the Taliban?" *Small Wars and Insurgencies*, Vol. 21, No. 2, June 2012, pp. 404–408.

Miles, Donna, "Panetta Discusses Defense Issues on '60 Minutes,'" American Forces Press Service, January 30, 2012. As of October 4, 2013: http://www.defense.gov/News/NewsArticle.aspx?ID=66977

Miller, Paul D., "The US and Afghanistan After 2014," *Survival*, Vol. 55, No. 1, February–March 2013, pp. 87–102.

Mockaitis, Thomas R., *Resolving Insurgencies*, Carlisle, Pa.: Strategic Studies Institute, U.S. Army War College, June 2011.

Moloney, Ed, *A Secret History of the IRA*, New York: W. W. Norton and Company, 2002.

Mumford, Andrew, *Puncturing the Counterinsurgency Myth: Britain and Irregular Warfare in the Past, Present, and Future*, Carlisle, Pa.: Strategic Studies Institute, U.S. Army War College, September 2011.

Nation, R. Craig, *War in the Balkans, 1991–2002*, Carlisle, Pa.: Strategic Studies Institute, U.S. Army War College, August 2003.

Nordland, Rod, and Alissa J. Rubin, "Taliban's Divided Tactics Raise Doubts Over Talks," *New York Times*, June 25, 2013.

Novosel, Tony, *Northern Ireland's Lost Opportunity: The Frustrated Promise of Political Loyalism*, London: Pluto Press, 2013.

Nugent, Paul, *Africa Since Independence: A Comparative History*, New York: Palgrave Macmillan, 2004.

Nye, Joseph S., Jr., *Soft Power: The Means to Success in World Politics*, New York: PublicAffairs, 2004.

Oliker, Olga, *Russia's Chechen Wars 1994–2000: Lessons from Urban Combat*, Santa Monica, Calif.: RAND Corporation, MR-1289-A, 2001. As of October 4, 2013: http://www.rand.org/pubs/monograph_reports/MR1289.html

Paul, Christopher, Colin P. Clarke, and Beth Grill, *Victory Has a Thousand Fathers: Detailed Counterinsurgency Case Studies*, Santa Monica, Calif.: RAND Corporation, MG-964/1-OSD, 2010a. As of October 4, 2013: http://www.rand.org/pubs/monographs/MG964z1.html

———, *Victory Has a Thousand Fathers: Sources of Success in Counterinsurgency*, Santa Monica, Calif.: RAND Corporation, MG-964-OSD, 2010b. As of October 4, 2013: http://www.rand.org/pubs/monographs/MG964.html

Paul, Christopher, Colin P. Clarke, Beth Grill, and Molly Dunigan, *Counterinsurgency Scorecard: Afghanistan in Early 2013 Relative to Insurgencies Since World War II*, Santa Monica, Calif.: RAND Corporation, RR-396-OSD, 2013a. As of October 4, 2013:
http://www.rand.org/pubs/research_reports/RR396.html

———, *Paths to Victory: Detailed Insurgency Case Studies*, Santa Monica, Calif.: RAND Corporation, RR-291/2-OSD, 2013b. As of October 4, 2013:
http://www.rand.org/pubs/research_reports/RR291z2.html

———, *Paths to Victory: Lessons from Modern Insurgencies*, Santa Monica, Calif.: RAND Corporation, RR-291/1-OSD, 2013c. As of October 4, 2013:
http://www.rand.org/pubs/research_reports/RR291z1.html

Picard, Elizabeth, *Lebanon: A Shattered Country*, New York: Holmes and Meier, 2002.

Pruitt, Dean G., "Negotiation with Terrorists," *International Negotiation*, Vol. 11, No. 2, 2006, pp. 371–394.

Reyntjens, Filip, "Briefing: Burundi: A Peaceful Transition After a Decade of War?" *African Affairs*, Vol. 105, No. 418, January 2006, pp. 117–135.

Rudolph, Rachel M., "Transition in the Philippines: The Moro National Liberation Front (MNLF), the Moro Islamic Liberation Front (MILF) and Abu Sayyaf's Group (ASG)," in Anisseh Van Engeland and Rachel M. Rudolph, *From Terrorism to Politics*, Burlington, Vt.: Ashgate, 2008, pp. 151–170.

Ruttig, Thomas, *The Battle for Afghanistan: Negotiations with the Taliban*, Washington, D.C.: New America Foundation, May 2011.

Saunders, Harold H., "Sustained Dialogue in Managing Intractable Conflict," *Negotiation Journal*, Vol. 19, No. 1, January 2003, pp. 85–95.

Sederberg, Peter C., "Conciliation as Counter-Terrorist Strategy," *Journal of Peace Research*, Vol. 32, No. 3, August 1995, pp. 295–312.

Semple, Michael, *Reconciliation in Afghanistan*, Washington, D.C.: United States Institute of Peace, 2009.

Shinn, James, and James Dobbins, *Afghan Peace Talks: A Primer*, Santa Monica, Calif.: RAND Corporation, MG-1131-RC, 2011. As of October 4, 20113:
http://www.rand.org/pubs/monographs/MG1131.html

Shultz, Richard H., Jr., and Andrea Dew, *Insurgents, Terrorists, and Militias: The Warriors of Contemporary Combat*, New York: Columbia University Press, 2006.

Silber, Laura, and Alan Little, *Yugoslavia: Death of a Nation*, New York: Penguin Books, 1995.

Sisk, Timothy D., *Power Sharing and International Mediation in Ethnic Conflicts*, Washington, D.C.: United States Institute of Peace, 1996.

Smith, M. L. R., and Peter R. Neumann, "Motorman's Long Journey: Changing the Strategic Setting in Northern Ireland," *Contemporary British History*, Vol. 19, No. 4, December 2005, pp. 413–435.

Smith, R. Grant, "Tajikistan: The Rocky Road to Peace," *Central Asian Survey*, Vol. 18, No. 2, 1999, pp. 243–251.

Stanekzai, Mohammad Masoom, *Thwarting Afghanistan's Insurgency: A Pragmatic Approach Toward Peace and Reconciliation*, Washington, D.C.: United States Institute of Peace, September 2008.

Staniland, Paul, "Defeating Transnational Insurgencies: The Best Offense Is a Good Fence," *Washington Quarterly*, Vol. 29, No. 1, Winter 2005–2006, pp. 21–40.

Stedman, Stephen John, "Spoiler Problems in Peace Processes," *International Security*, Vol. 22, No. 2, Fall 1997, pp. 5–53.

Stryker, Robin, "Beyond History Versus Theory: Strategic Narrative and Sociological Explanation," *Sociological Methods and Research*, Vol. 24, No. 3, February 1996, pp. 304–352.

"Text of Bush Middle East Speech," ABC News, April 4, 2002. As of August 2013:
http://abcnews.go.com/International/story?id=80034

Thom, William G., *African Wars: A Defense Intelligence Perspective*, Calgary, Alb.: University of Calgary Press, 2010.

Toft, Monica Duffy, *Securing the Peace: The Durable Settlement of Civil Wars*, Princeton, N.J.: Princeton University Press, 2009.

Toros, Harmonie, "'We Don't Negotiate with Terrorists!' Legitimacy and Complexity in Terrorist Conflicts," *Security Dialogue*, Vol. 49, No. 4, August 2008, pp. 407–426.

Tull, Denis M., and Andreas Mehler, "The Hidden Costs of Power-Sharing: Reproducing Insurgent Violence in Africa," *African Affairs*, Vol. 104, No. 416, July 2005, pp. 375–378.

U.S. Department of Defense, *Report on Progress Toward Security and Stability in Afghanistan*, Washington, D.C., April 2012. As of October 4, 2013:
http://www.defense.gov/news/1230_Report_final.pdf

Waldman, Matt, *Dangerous Liaisons with the Afghan Taliban: The Feasibility and Risks of Negotiation*, Washington, D.C.: United States Institute of Peace, Special Report No. 256, October 2010.

Walter, Barbara F., *The Successful Settlement of Civil Wars*, Princeton, N.J.: Princeton University Press, 2001.

Weinberg, Leonard, Ami Pedahzur, and Ari Perliger, *Political Parties and Terrorist Groups*, London: Routledge, 2009.

Witty, David M., "A Regular Army in Counterinsurgency Operations: Egypt in Yemen, 1962–1967," *Journal of Military History*, Vol. 65, No. 2, April 2001, pp. 401–440.

Woodward, Bob, *Obama's Wars*, New York: Simon and Schuster, 2010.

Zartman, I. William, ed., "Dynamics and Constraints in Negotiations in Internal Conflicts," in I. William Zartman, ed., *Elusive Peace: Negotiating an End to Civil Wars*, Washington, D.C.: Brookings Institution Press, 1995, pp. 3–30.

Zunes, Stephen, and Jacob Mundy, *Western Sahara: War, Nationalism, and Conflict Irresolution*, Syracuse, N.Y.: Syracuse University Press, 2010.